Computer Secrets
I Taught My Mom

Michael Shannon

SmartGuy Press

Notice of Liability

ISBN: 0-9773105-0-7

Trademarks

Unconditional Guarantee

Dedicated To My Wonderful Mother,

Louise.

Thanks for all your support!

Acknowledgments

Thanks to my extraordinary wife Laura. This book would not have been possible without your love and support over the last five years.

Thanks also to my magnificent friends and family! Val, Sherri, David, Sharon, Dot, Rosemary, Lance and Nicole, Anne and Jack, Sharon and Ron, Dick and Marcy, Randy and Toni.

Table of Contents

Introduction

Most people who are "comfortable" using a PC learned by the worst way possible; memorization. Someone showing you a rote series of movements is not teaching you the underlying concepts you need to truly "get it". The majority of computer books on the market attempt to teach using this memorization method.

There has to be a better way – and there is! To truly understand how to use a PC involves understanding a relatively small number of "core concepts". Learn these and you'll be able to figure out how to install hardware, resolve technical issues, and use any software.

Using a PC, despite what you've heard or read, is a relatively simple skill to acquire. Anyone can do it. If you can read and follow instructions, you'll quickly realize just how easy it is. The first step is to know that you can acquire this skill. And make no mistake, you can!

My mom was a total neophyte who initially believed that the word "RAM" could mean only one thing – a large hoofed mammal native to western mountain ranges.[*] Today however, she is a computer master with a high-speed Internet connection who starts everyday by reading her e-mail.

You might be surprised how few "techies" or "computer geeks" truly understand the real basics of computers. As it turns out, my experience has shown the need for a different kind of computer teaching book. One that doesn't necessarily

---

[*] In case **you're** a total neophyte, RAM in computer lingo, is an acronym for Random Access Memory, the basic memory used in personal computers. More on that later.

rely on memorization of icons, menus, and endless computer jargon, but instead teaches the fundamental, core concepts that will lead anyone to total mastery of the PC. **You can learn to use a PC! And you will become an expert in a relatively short period of time.**

As a former corporate programmer and technical support analyst, many friends and family members regularly consult with me on computer issues and questions. They are frequently amazed that I consistently solve their problems even though I have little or no experience with the specific issues they are experiencing. I am happy to let these folks think I am a genius, or perhaps even a computer magician, but the fact is that over the many years of playing and working with computers, I've learned that almost every single situation can be addressed by following a few simple rules and concepts. This is a wonderful thing and quite necessary as there are too many types of hardware and software, as well as thousands of other variables that make it impossible for anyone to memorize everything.

Consider driving a car. You open the door, you sit on the seat and pull the seatbelt over your shoulder for safety. You then start the engine, and place the car in gear. These actions are understood by everyone who drives a car. There is no need to "relearn" or to figure out how these things are done when switching to a different vehicle. A solid core understanding allows you to select a gear regardless of where the gear lever is because you understand the function of that device. A computer is no different!

Computers seem very complex and complicated to the uninitiated. Though there are many options and variables, we can boil down using a PC to a relatively small number of core concepts. No matter what the task is you want to accomplish or what the problem is that you're experiencing, there are only a finite number of ways of interacting with the computer. Most computer interaction consists of nothing more than a keyboard, mouse and display – that's it! And, there are only a finite number of things you can do with a keyboard and mouse.

Those things are:

● Type – enter text

● Point at something

● Point at something and a click a mouse button one or more times (called, not surprisingly, "pointing and clicking")

● Point at something, hold down a mouse button, then move the mouse (known as "dragging" and also as "selecting")

Now, you might be saying "Sure, but you have to know *what* to type and *where* to point and click." This is true, but again your options are limited. You won't have to learn or memorize all of these options. You only have to learn how to figure out which option is correct.

Read the above line again as it's vitally important. The gist of this book is simple:

● Learn how to interact with the PC

● Learn how and where to find things – navigation

● Get the "big picture"

● Make the correct choice

Learning to use a PC is a lot like exploring a huge, old mansion or a hospital. It's a large space with lots of nooks and crannies, but the general layout makes sense once you understand it. At first, you're totally overwhelmed. Once you "get" the general layout of the place, you become comfortable and can find your way around even if you can't specifically remember where a room is. Unfortunately, many fledgling computer users never take the short time required to learn the overall scheme of things. They simply want to learn how to perform a specific task.

If you are patient enough to read and apply the information contained in this book, you will eventually "get it". It can be a steep learning curve, particularly for older adults. Their preconceived notions and inability to associate everyday tasks with what takes place on the computer is a common downfall. With effort comes results. You will reach that "AAHaaa!" moment when everything comes together and you become an expert.

I would ask you to put aside your preconceived notions of what you think or have heard or read about using a PC. In essence, forget everything you know about computers, and start from here.

In this book we'll primarily focus on Windows XP. This is the operating system, the core software of the computer, which controls all basic computer functions. Other operating systems exist, though none are quite as popular as Windows.

In spite of being popular, Windows XP comes with little or no documentation. Users are apparently supposed to absorb the information they need out of thin air...hence, the need for this type of book.

If you already own a computer, chances are good it runs Windows. If you are going to be purchasing a new computer system, you'll probably want to buy one with the Windows operating system. Though a Macintosh, while more expensive, is also a good choice.

If you do happen to come across a computer with a different operating system, you won't be totally lost after reading this book. Most of the "big picture" concepts explained here apply regardless of the operating system.

Conventions Used In This Book

Watch for secrets. These are indicated by the "Top Secret" graphic and **bold text.**

Pay special attention to these areas! You won't find this information anywhere else and it is crucial for a thorough understanding.*

Some may seem trivial and common sense, but master these and you will master the computer.

In the many examples included throughout the book you will see commands in quotes. Don't actually type the quotes when trying these yourself. For example, a line might read:

At the blinking cursor, type "format".

In this case you would only type the word format, not the quotes.

*   Ok, that's a bit of an exaggeration, but the bold "**Top Secret**" text highlights important points.

Throughout the book you may notice that I make occasional generalizations, such as "generally", "mostly", "usually", "almost always" and similar less than definitive words and phrases.

Due to the peculiarities of the computer industry, there is just no way to be 100% certain, especially when discussing computers and applications in general.

My goal with this book is not to teach you the specific details of an application or inner workings of the XP operating system. Instead, I want to instill in you a unique way of thinking about using computers and software.

I've done my best to explain things as accurately as possible. If an explanation contained herein does not work for your particular situation, hopefully the general knowledge contained here will allow you to think through the problem.

You'll find in some cases that I've repeated definitions or explanations in multiple areas. This is by design as certain topics are pertinent to other topics. This repetition also reinforces major points.

Note: If by some stroke of luck you already own a computer, you may wish to just peruse the first portion of Chapter 1, which explains the basic parts of a computer, skip the portion on buying, and dive right into Chapter 2, "The Mouse and Keyboard".

The computer industry moves at an extraordinary pace. What is popular, relevant and accurate today, may well be none of those things six months from now. Major updates and error corrections will appear in future printings of this book. In the meantime, be sure and periodically check www.smartguypress.com and click on "Book Updates" for any late breaking information.

Oh, and one other thing! I am always interested in hearing about errors, omissions, or just your opinions on the book. Feel free to e-mail me (you'll be learning how to do this very soon) at computersecrets@smartguypress.com.

I can't guarantee I'll be able to answer every message, but all will be read and appreciated.

And finally – Thank you very much for purchasing this book!

Chapter 1
What is a PC?

It seems like every time you turn around, every sub-culture in America is making up their own language. The computer industry is certainly one of the worst for creating nonsensical jargon that puts many people off. Confusing and complex sounding terms cause many, perhaps even yourself, to "shutdown" when reading or hearing this incomprehensible babble. Even veterans of the industry are not immune to this phenomenon.

TOP SECRET **Remember this: Most computer jargon is simply invented terms used to describe new technology. Don't be put off by technobabble. A bit of research and common sense will show that even the most intimidating geek-speak is easy to understand.**

Here is a perfect example and a true story: Upon returning from vacation to my job as a systems administrator, I was perusing my backlog of e-mail when I came to a message from my boss. The e-mail read "Please see Bill about the upcoming e-commerce technology refresh initiative he is leading." Now at this point I had worked in the industry for well over a dozen years, yet I had absolutely no idea what this phrase "e-commerce technology refresh initiative" could mean. So, I approached Bill to inquire about what exactly was going on. "Oh that! Yea, we're replacing the two web server computers with newer, faster ones." I responded, "So we're getting two new computers, and you titled the project the e-commerce technology refresh initiative?!?" To which Bill said, "Yea, sounds important, don't you think?" "You don't want to know what I really think, Pal..."

And that my friends, is really the heart of the matter – when it comes time to name something, make it difficult to understand and complex sounding and people will think you're smart and important. Now there is a lesson for the kids! Watch "The Apprentice" to see this concept in action.

There is good news however! You really need to learn and understand very little computer jargon to successfully use a PC. And once you open your mind, you'll see that most computer jargon is simply words you haven't heard before that describe very simple things or processes.

Before we can talk about how to learn to use a PC, we have to know a bit about what a PC, short for Personal Computer, actually is. Let's take a general look at this and then a more specific look at what to buy if you're in the market for a PC. I'll also introduce the first of several analogies to keep in mind when learning to use a PC. These are visual analogies to help relate the use of a PC to real-life non-computer tasks that virtually everyone can relate to.

For example, think of a computer hard disk, the device which stores computer information, as nothing more than a file cabinet found in any office. Everyone can understand how a file cabinet works. I am consistently amazed at the number of seemingly experienced users who "lose" files. They "lose" these files simply because they don't understand the underlying concepts of the file system. Learn the "file cabinet" analogy and you'll never lose a file. Thinking in these terms will allow you to grasp the "big picture" of using a PC. Keep these analogies in your mind when working on a PC. When you have trouble or are stuck, think about the analogy and how you might resolve the issue in that context.

I am not going to go in to a lot of detail about how computers function or their history. Somewhere near the front of every non-fiction book you read is the "History of" whatever the book is about. Usually the reader has little or no interest in this information. As an author, I have to make assumptions about you, the reader. My first assumption is that you really don't care much about the history of personal computing. My second assumption is that you really don't care exactly how computers do the things they do. You just want to know how to make a computer do what you want it to. You don't have to understand how electronic fuel injection works to drive your car, right?

Hardware Basics

There are two main types of PCs; desktop and laptop, the latter also referred to as notebook. You'll occasionally hear of a third type, server, but this is simply a variation of the desktop type and is used mainly by businesses .

Desktop PCs are usually composed of several separate pieces. The main CPU (central processing unit) or box, is the actual "computer" and houses the main computing chips and other peripherals we will discuss later. The monitor, also referred to as the "display", is the screen of the computer and is the main visual output – this is the "TV" of the computer. The keyboard and mouse are attached to the CPU and are the main source of input to the computer. There also may be speakers attached to the CPU for sound output. In addition, any number of additional peripherals may be connected to the computer by cables, such as external drives, printers, and scanners.

Notebook, or laptop PCs are "all-in-one" designs. They feature a clamshell design in which the CPU, display, drives, speakers and keyboard are all integrated into one unit. They also contain one or more batteries which allows the notebook PC to be used away from a dedicated power source for up to several hours depending on the number and type of batteries. It can also be plugged in to a wall for long term use and battery recharging.

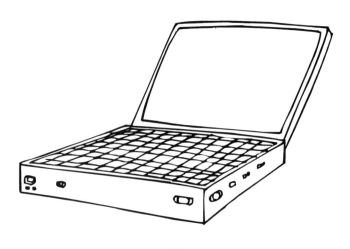

Regardless of whether a PC is a desktop or a laptop, it consists of the same basic components. Let's take a look at each component in detail. It isn't necessary to memorize these parts or have a thorough understanding of how each works, but a simple overview will help you with the big picture. A basic knowledge of these items will also prove useful when continuing your PC education by reading computer-related books and magazines.

- **CPU – Central Processing Unit**. This is the main processing chip of the computer where all of the number crunching and instruction interpreting is handled. Most computers also have additional processors for specific operations such as video/graphics, floating-point math, and sound. Popular processors are produced by AMD and Intel. These processors are rated by speed, in terms of gigahertz (GHz) – with faster being better and more expensive.

- **Hard Drive or Hard Disk –** This is where all of the information is *stored* on a computer. And here is our first concept that you will need to learn – all information on a computer is stored in files. Now there are many different kinds of files; music, graphic, executables (programs or applications, more about that later), and many others. No matter what anyone tells you though, everything on a computer is a type of file, and that file is stored somewhere, usually on a hard disk. Disks are rated by the amount of information they hold. This rating is in gigabytes (GB). A gigabyte is defined as 1024 megabytes, which probably means nothing to you. Without giving too technical an explanation, a typical file stored on a disk averages less than 1 MB, though files can be any size. If you're purchasing a system, look for at least a 30-40 GB hard disk which will allow you to store thousands of files.

There are various types of disks, see "Additional Drives" below.

- **RAM – Random Access Memory**. This is the computer's main memory. Basically, this is an area where files are held temporarily (*not* stored; a significant difference which confuses many people) while the computer is operating. RAM is a specific kind of electronic chip. There may be other types of memory used in a computer, such as for graphics or sound. The amount of RAM installed in a PC is expressed in MB or GB; megabytes or gigabytes. With RAM, more is always better. Currently most systems come with 256mb which is sufficient, while 512 mb or even 1gb (gigabyte) is even better.

- **Monitor or Display (for desktop computers)** – For lack of a better description, this is the "TV" of the computer used to display all visual information. For desktop PCs, there are several options. Until just recently the most popular option, called a "CRT" for Cathode Ray Tube, looked and performed much like a normal TV. Now the trend is definitely toward flat-screen LCD, Liquid Crystal Display, and plasma displays which have the advantage of being much thinner and lighter. Notebooks have an integral display which is typically a type of LCD. For a desktop PC, flat-panel LCD and plasma displays have come down in price so much in the last five years that it would be difficult *not* to recommend one. A 17" monitor is totally adequate for most computing and will run around $300-$400. Bigger is generally better in this case, but price escalates rapidly, and larger screens are really only a necessity for graphic arts, CAD, and intense action games. Get a CRT (old-style monitor that resembles a TV) only if you are very strapped for cash. A 17" CRT can be had for less than $200.

- **Laptop Display** – The display for a laptop is built into the computer itself, you still have several choices however. When buying or configuring a notebook PC first look at display size. A 15" notebook display was, until very recently, considered huge. Today, 15.4" is very common with 17" as an option. Dell, a popular mail-order PC seller, is rumored to be releasing a 19" screen in early 2006. Keep in mind that as display size goes up, portability goes down. Regardless of the size you get (go for 15" or above), get a display with one of the new screen "brightening" technologies. Several companies offer this as an option such as HP/Compaq's Brightview, and Sony's Xbrite. These technologies brighten the screen considerably, as well as increase the angle from which the screen can be viewed.

- **Mouse or Pointing Device** – Several varieties are available, including wireless, which reduces clutter on the desktop by eliminating the cable. If you have the choice, opt for an "optical" mouse. These have no moving parts and can't get clogged with dust, lint and piles of cat hair like roller ball mice. A laptop's pointing devices are built in to the computer itself and usually consist of a touchpad with two or more buttons. Regardless of type or style, these devices allow the user to move a cursor, also called a pointer, on the screen, and also to click objects via buttons.

- **Additional Drives or Storage Devices** – Most modern PCs have at least one additional drive. In the past, this was most likely a "floppy" drive, which used 3.5" removable plastic disks for storage. Now, most computers have a CD drive, which uses compact disks for storage. CD-ROM drives can only read from the disks. This is still useful as most software is distributed on CD. CD-R or CD-RW drives can both read and write as well, thus allowing you to save your files to inexpensive compact disks.

- **Keyboard** – The keyboard is the "typewriter" portion of the computer that along with the mouse, combine to allow input to the computer. Now this is an important concept: to successfully use a computer, you must interact with it. This is accomplished by using the mouse and the keyboard – that's it! There are additional ways of getting information into and out of the computer but all computer/human interaction is done via the mouse and keyboard. Remember this. As you progress through this book, you not only want to learn the specific "hows and whys" of using a PC, but more importantly you'll want to learn how to "think" about using a computer so you'll be able to figure things out for yourself. The first step is above, so I'll repeat it one more time for clarity: all computer/human interaction is done via the mouse and keyboard. So, when you think about what it means to use a computer, you are simply sitting in front of the display using the keyboard and mouse.

Again, it's not vital that you understand how all these pieces work, but it is important that you have a general understanding of the flow of information through a computer. Luckily, this is very simple.

Files, lists containing information, stored on one or more drives, are loaded into RAM, where the various processing chips (CPUs) use whatever information they need from the files. The input the user provides through the keyboard and the mouse determine what files are loaded, used, and processed.

26

A common problem among PC users, even experienced users, is confusing RAM with hard disk space. This confusion generally arises as both items are expressed in terms of size in megabytes (MB) or gigabytes (GB).

Here's an easy way to visualize and distinguish the difference: think of a disk as a storage place where files are saved *permanently*, whether the computer is on or off. Visualize a file cabinet in an office with several drawers. The number of drawers determines the size of the cabinet and its capacity for storage.

Think of RAM as a place where files are *temporarily* held, and only when the computer is powered on. Visualize the number of folders you could remove from the file cabinet and hold in your hand. Obviously this is a much smaller amount than you could store in the filing cabinet. And indeed, the amount of RAM is usually much smaller than the amount of disk storage. A typical PC might have 40-100 GB of disk storage and only 256 MB-1 GB of RAM. (256MB is .25GB; 1000 MB = 1 GB)

Software

Ever hear the witticism "There are two kinds of people in the world? Those that divide people in to groups and those who don't?" Well, computer software is much like that. We could break it up into an endless number of groupings, but initially, let's keep it simple and list only two groups; operating system software, and everything else, which we'll call "applications" or "programs".

Software, as opposed to the hardware we just discussed, contains the instructions for the computer. It's called "soft" as there is nothing to physically touch. Think of software as a list of instructions. Now, these lists are kept in files, and files must be stored on something. And this "something" is, in fact physical, and can be touched, like a hard disk or compact disk. Consider the old-style equivalent of computer files and folders: a piece of paper and a file folder.

TOP SECRET **Everything stored on a PC is a file! These files are nothing more than containers for information. Whether it's being described as software, a word processing document, spreadsheet, picture, music or web page, everything is a file and all files are stored somewhere. That "somewhere" is most likely a hard disk, but could be a CD, DVD, floppy disk, or even just the computer's memory (RAM), if it hasn't been "saved" yet. Whatever you create on your computer – letters, e-mails, graphics, or music files – are known as "data files"; files where your data is stored. If you create something, such as a letter, you must save it! If you do not save it, which means permanently storing it, your work will be gone as soon as you exit the application or turn off the PC!**

Operating System

As we've just learned, software is a list of instructions that the hardware of the computer uses to function. The base software is the Operating System or just "OS". This special software controls the hardware, provides the user interface (more in a bit), and allows application software to function. The operating system software on over 90% of all PCs is some version of Microsoft's Windows. Other options include Apple's OS X, which requires special, proprietary hardware, and various flavors of Unix, such as the up-and-coming Linux. Generally, new PCs come with an operating system, usually the latest version of Windows, already installed. Turn the computer on and you're ready to go.

The user interface, often called "GUI" (pronounced "gooey") or graphical user interface, allows the user to interact with the computer. Many years ago, computer user interfaces had no graphics at all and simply consisted of a screen and cursor where text commands were typed.

This type of interface, called a "command line interface", required the user to memorize exact commands and still exists today on many computer systems. In fact, Windows has a legacy command line interface called DOS that can be used at any time. Luckily, the *need* to use it is rare.

Graphical user interfaces use a pointing device (mouse) to interact with windows, icons, menus and the Desktop. Occasionally you will see GUIs referred to as "WIMP interfaces" – windows, mouse, menu, and pointer interfaces. This is from "back in the day" when GUIs were sneered upon by "real" computer geeks who would only use the command line interface.

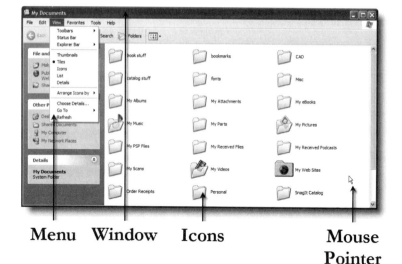

Menu   Window   Icons   Mouse Pointer

Icons are small graphics that represent something. Remember that everything is a file? Well, what icons represent, in the context of computers, are files. Icons are not an invention of the computer industry.

In fact, you'll find icons everywhere. For example, most automobiles are loaded with icons on their various switches and knobs. And everyone is familiar with this icon:

Once you become familiar with the user interface, icons are relatively easy to understand even if you don't know precisely what they represent because you'll understand the context in which they are used.

For example, take a look at the following graphic.

Recycle Bin

This is the Recycle Bin icon that resides on the Windows Desktop. Now, even if you know nothing about computers, you probably know what a Recycle Bin is – you put something in it that you no longer want. In this particular instance, Microsoft is apparently being politically correct. On Apple computers, this icon is labeled "Trash", which is much closer to the truth as no recycling is actually done.

Menus are lists of commands with each line of the list being a choice. So, menus are nothing more than lists of choices or options.

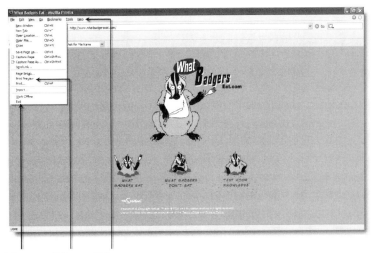

Menu   Menu   Menu
          Item   Bar

Windows (the generic term, not the operating system itself) are graphical containers. These are the "frames" or "rectangles" that contain icons, menus, toolbars and work areas for applications. There are two kinds of windows. Those belonging to the Windows OS itself are called Explorer windows. Those which contain workspaces for specific applications are called application windows. The significance and confusion of this will become apparent in Chapter 4.

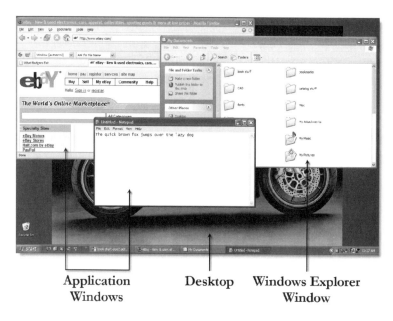

Application Windows	Desktop	Windows Explorer Window

When a PC is up and running, the screen that appears is the Desktop. This Windows Desktop is much like the desktop of any office desk – a place to work. Files can be placed on the Desktop, and applications (software tools that let you do various kinds of work) can be opened on the Desktop just like a "real" desktop. The Desktop is an important area and essentially where all your computing activities will be started.

TOP SECRET The Desktop is a good analogy, though referring to it as a workbench may be better. PCs are so supremely capable and flexible today that many of the tasks they can now perform have no direct analogy to anything associated with a real desk or office. A good example of such a task would be writing a custom playlist of music to a compact disk. So it may be helpful to envision a workbench, where virtually anything you can dream of can be accomplished. This area, the Desktop, is your home base – you'll start here every time you do something on the PC and come back here again and again.*

Application Software

Application software, called applications, apps, or just programs, are the tools used to accomplish specific tasks. While the operating system concerns itself with handling the hardware and user interface, applications are concerned with very specific tasks such as word processing, spreadsheets, playing music and videos, or browsing web pages.

TOP SECRET Here's another case of computer jargon gone horribly awry. The phrase "word processing" brings about visions of complex calculations involving arcane and exotic languages. In fact, this phrase points to nothing more than an application used for typing. Write a letter? Create an invitation? Make a lost dog sign to hang in your neighborhood? Yup, you'll use a word processing application.

---

* As a quick aside, several years ago Commodore's Amiga computer system did use the "workbench" term and analogy for its GUI. Sadly, though popular, Commodore went bankrupt a few years later.

Applications are generally specific to an operating system. So, a word processor that works with Microsoft Windows will not work on an Apple Macintosh. Versions of applications usually exist for multiple operating systems. Make sure when installing a new application that it is specifically intended for your operating system.

The Flow

Do you need to know how your television works in order to watch Survivor on Thursday night? Thought not. As long as you can work the remote, and for men that's a genetic capability, you're good to go.

The complex inner workings of computers – hardware and software – are beyond the scope of this book.[*] However, a general overview will help you to understand the "big picture" as you progress through your journey of learning.

In greater detail, here's what happens when you turn on the power:

- Preprogrammed instructions from ROM (Read Only Memory; instructions permanently stored on chips) are carried out by the CPU, such as how to access disk drives, and what information to load into RAM.

- Operating system software (Windows) stored on the hard disk begins to load necessary instructions into RAM – this is called "booting". As in, "hold on, I am booting my PC".

[*]   After completing this book you'll have the skills and knowledge to get online. Once there, you may want to surf on over to www.howstuffworks.com. You'll find not only dozens of articles on the inner workings of computers, but everything else you can imagine. A good website I highly recommend.

Even though the power is on, the PC is not ready for use until the boot process completes. This can take a few minutes.

- The CPU relays user input to OS, reading and writing information from hard disk as needed.

Buying A PC

If you as yet don't have a PC, but are in the market for one, you may be intimidated by the seemingly overwhelming options and variables. Don't despair; it's easy to narrow down the options and make a decision that is right for you.

First, decide whether you would like a desktop or laptop style of PC.

Desktop PCs are typically less expensive, offer greater expandability/upgradability, and the flexibility to connect various sized displays. The downsides are lack of mobility and size.

Laptop, or notebook computers, main claim to fame is their portability. You can take a notebook virtually anywhere and, with the advent of wireless networking, grab an Internet connection from virtually anywhere, including around your house or even at the local Starbuck's. The downsides are a relatively small display area, and inability to upgrade individual hardware parts later on. In addition, notebooks tend to be a few steps behind desktop computers in terms of performance. The CPUs and graphics cards used in notebooks are not quite as fast as those used in desktop PCs. This probably won't be noticeable to most users unless your primary focus is playing the latest games.

The best advice is to make your choice based on mobility. If you can live with your PC being in one place, then a desktop is definitely the way to go. You'll save money and get a higher performance machine. If you'd like to use your computer in different locations, perhaps the kitchen or the the den, as well as take advantage of all the available wireless "hotspots", get a laptop.

The next decision you'll need to make is where you will purchase your new PC. Your two choices are mail-order, or from a retail establishment. Don't even consider buying a used computer until you know exactly what you're doing.

Personally, I like mail-order. It's easy to customize the PC exactly to my needs and is generally less expensive. In addition it is also possible to save the sales tax cost. You also avoid dealing with the retail salespeople telling you that the sky will fall and life on earth will end if you don't purchase the extended warranty. Of course, you do have to know what you want when buying via mail order. And since you're probably not online yet (since you don't have a computer) you'll need to actually call the computer companies like Dell, Gateway, and HP/Compaq. Check recent issues of PC World magazine for advertisements and rankings of current computer models. Some people are simply more comfortable walking into a store to make their purchase and being able to take the item back locally if a problem arises.

If you do buy at a local store, your choices are usually limited to pre-configured stock on hand. Not necessarily a bad thing, but it does limit your choices somewhat.

Regardless of where you choose to make your purchase, decline the extended service warranty no matter what they say. Most electronic items with inherent manufacturing defects will fail almost immediately. This typically occurs within the manufacturer's warranty period. Decline extended warranties on all items you purchase, save the money and when something breaks, repair or replace it. You'll still come out ahead in the long run.

Also decline to purchase expensive and unneeded add-ons at the time of purchase. PC systems generally come with everything you need to get started (except for this book). The only exception to this being a printer cable if you purchase a printer separately. Retailers like to push expensive surge protectors, mouse pads, virus/spyware programs, and long-term Internet contracts at the time of purchase. Decline. You can always purchase these items as needed later. Also, there is no need for a fancy surge protector. In more than 20 years of using computers, I've never seen or heard of a PC damaged by a power surge, lightning, or any other type of electrical event. I am not saying it's impossible, just unlikely. Any inexpensive outlet strip will work just fine.

Setting It All Up

I am very cheap and not fond of paying others to do tasks I know I could do if I just expend a bit of effort. Occasionally it's worth it though. If you're a complete novice to computing and have just purchased a system, your best bet is to have someone knowledgeable help you with the initial set-up. Sometimes this just isn't possible though, and if that is the case ,you'll be able to muddle through it with the help of this book.

Ideally, you can get help from a family member or friend with PC experience. Bake them some cookies or buy them some beer. If you can't find a willing person, set up the computer system yourself by following the "quick start" guide included with almost every system sold today. Then pay an installer to hook up a high-speed Internet connection. (See the Chapter 6 for more on this)

Once you get the pieces of the PC connected (if it is a desktop), follow the quickstart guide to power up the PC. The power button usually has a circle with a line through it or an "I/O" type symbol. In case you're wondering, this is a graphic representation of 1 and 0, binary for on and off.

Computers are not like lamps – they don't instantly turn on and off with a flick of a switch. Pressing the power switch simply initiates the "boot" process which takes a minute or two.

The first time you boot up a Windows PC, it will display boxes that ask you to answer various questions to initially configure Windows. As a complete rookie you might not have these answers. That's perfectly fine. Answer what you can and skip the remainder. Use the mouse to select the "Next" and "OK" buttons to proceed as needed. (See Chapter 2 for more) At the end of this setup interview, you'll be asked to set up accounts for users of the PC. For the time being, create only one account for the main user, probably yourself. Rest assured that you will be able to add or change any of the requested information later on.

TOP SECRET Looking to buy a PC? First, decide whether you want a desktop or notebook PC. Get a copy of the latest issue of PC World magazine. PC World has lists of computer hardware sorted by ranking. Note the type of hardware, specifically the CPU the top PCs have and compare this to ads in the magazine. Select a system a step or two back from the cutting edge – which generally means the most expensive. The most expensive PCs utilize the latest technology, but you'll definitely have a lighter wallet and you probably won't notice the difference. Don't worry too much about expandability or upgradability. It's often easier and cheaper to upgrade the whole system in a few years. This way, you avoid the hassle of trying to get various parts and pieces to work together. When you upgrade the entire system you also receive the latest version of the Windows operating system.

Chapter 2

The Mouse and Keyboard

The Mouse

So, you're sitting in front of your newly purchased PC with mouse in hand, wondering exactly what you're going to do next. The answer is *not* to pick it up by the wire and slam it on the floor. Although this is a common instinct among most budding computer enthusiasts, plastic shards can blind you.

Let's examine the mouse in detail and learn how to use this little beast without inflicting any bodily harm – at least to yourself.

Mice consist of two main parts: the part you move, which in turn moves the cursor on the screen, and the buttons. Most mice have two buttons, defined as left and right. Some mice have a third button or small wheel usually located between the left and right buttons. The function of this third button is to allow for an alternate way of scrolling.* If your mouse does

---

* Notebooks computers have their mice built-in to the computer itself. Technically this is called a "pointing device". The external unit of the mouse, is instead, replaced by a touchpad used by dragging your finger across it. Regardless of the pointing device, the same left and right

have a third button, ignore it for now and concentrate on the left and right buttons only.

TOP SECRET **There is usually more than one way to accomplish any given task on a PC. And when it comes to Microsoft products, there are usually just shy of a billion ways to do any particular task. This, um, "feature" is renowned for creating confusion. Throughout this book I've tried to outline the clearest, and most popular methods for performing tasks. Keep in mind however that there are usually multiple methods. One is not necessarily better than another. Once you're comfortable with the basics, feel free to experiment and pick whatever works best for you!**

The mouse is the primary method of interacting with the PC. As was alluded to in the Introduction, there are only a few actions you can do with the mouse, but it's important that you get these burned into your memory with a hot poker.

Let's take an in-depth look at mousing around. Using a mouse really amounts to nothing more than moving the pointer (also called the cursor) on the screen to a specific spot by moving the mouse around your desk. Once at the required spot, your options are limited to:

- Pressing the left mouse button and letting it go quickly one or more times, called "clicking" or "left-clicking". Assume the generic "click" or "clicking" refers to the left mouse button.

buttons, as well as their connected actions, apply. For this book, I'll use the term "mouse" to refer to a pointing device. Oh, and most notebook computers also have a port where you can plug in a normal, handheld mouse should you prefer that.

- Pressing and continuing to press the left mouse button while moving the mouse is known as "dragging", "selecting", or "highlighting". It's nice when you can refer to something with three completely different words, don't you think?

- Pressing the right mouse button, called "right-clicking". Extremely useful and often overlooked, this is a cornerstone of the Windows architecture.

TOP SECRET The pointer, or cursor, (looks like an arrow) displayed onscreen is actually composed of two separate parts; the "hot spot" and the rest. The "hot spot" is the very tip of the cursor. It is very small, in fact one pixel.[*] If you experience problems clicking, selecting, or dragging on items, make sure that the mouse is positioned properly and you're using the very tip of the cursor, the hotspot. For example, when double-clicking on an icon, the hotspot must remain on the icon for both clicks.

Hot
Spot

The left mouse button is usually clicked with the index finger, though some users find it more comfortable to use both the index and middle finger. The number of required clicks depends upon what you're clicking on and where it is located.

- Icons located on the Desktop and within Explorer windows require two clicks.

[*] Pixel is an abbreviation of "picture element". It refers to a single dot that composes the display of a computer monitor or even a television.

- Icons on tool bars generally require one click.

- Menus require one click to display the menu and one click to select the menu item.

- Links or Hyperlinks, the fundamental navigation method of the World Wide Web (Internet), require only one click.

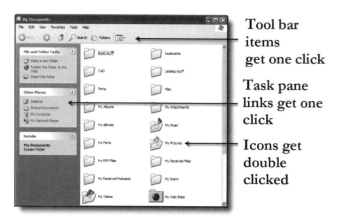

Tool bar items get one click

Task pane links get one click

Icons get double clicked

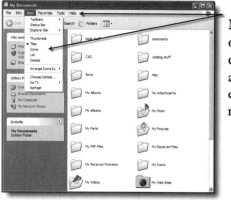

Menus require one click to display menu, and a second click to select menu item

TOP SECRET As you'll learn in future chapters, a core concept of using a PC is "selecting" an object, then performing an action on the selected object.

With this in mind there are a few secrets when it comes to selecting (also called "highlighting") text. And because you have to select text before you can do anything to it, it's worth spending the time to learn these shortcuts.

● Double-clicking a word selects the entire word

● If you keep the mouse button held down on the second click, you can drag the mouse horizontally and select text word-by-word instead of character-by-character.

● Triple-clicking selects the entire paragraph. With some applications, triple-clicking selects an entire line. With other programs, selecting a paragraph takes four clicks.

● Selecting a large portion of text, larger than will fit on the screen at one time, can be tricky. You could just start selecting and move the mouse to the top or bottom of the window. This will scroll the text, allowing you to continue selecting. However, it's tough to control the speed of the scrolling. Here is a better way: place the cursor by clicking at the beginning of the text you want to select. Then, using the scroll bar, navigate so that the end of the text you want to select is visible. Hold down the shift key and click at the end of the text – all the text in between the two clicks will become selected.

TOP SECRET Pay very close attention to the cursor. It can change shape and the shape can give you a hint as to the options available. For example, when you move the cursor (by default an arrow) to an area where you're expected to type something, the cursor changes to a text insertion cursor, which looks like an I-beam or flashing vertical line. To enter text in this area, just click and type. Likewise, when the cursor is moved over a web link, it turns into a hand with outstretched index finger indicating "click here". When dragging an object, the cursor may change to a circle with a slash through it, indicating that particular item can't be dropped there.

The right mouse button is usually pressed with the middle finger and is "clicked" - that is, pressed and released. This action displays a "context-sensitive menu". This means the operating system senses **where** you are right-clicking and displays a menu based on this location.

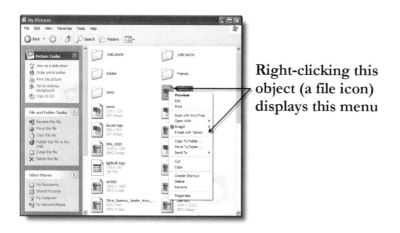

Right-clicking this object (a file icon) displays this menu

You right-click on objects. Those objects can be icons, selected text, cells in a spreadsheet, or graphics. Many different types of objects can be right-clicked on. Note that if an item does not have a context-menu available by right-clicking, nothing will happen if you try. Feel free to experiment, you won't break anything

Once a context-sensitive menu is displayed, the individual menu items are selected by a single left click.

TOP SECRET The right-click to display a context-sensitive menu is somewhat less than intuitive. Lots of users tend to forget about its existence. In fact, Microsoft research suggests that over 70% of users don't even use the right mouse button! According to software design standards, there should be an alternate way of doing things. However, this is not always the case, and some applications have tools and options that can only be accessed by right-clicking. Many times the context-sensitive menu contains "options", "properties", or "preferences" which allow you to change many settings. When in doubt, try it!

TOP SECRET The mouse cursor, the arrow that moves when you move the mouse, can be difficult to find and follow, particularly if you have a large display. If you'd like to make it easier to locate, try this: press the Windows key (has four wavy squares, (kind of looks like a flag to some people) usually located just to the side of the space bar). This displays the Start menu. Now press the letter "c" key. The control panel screen will open. Hold your mouse over "Printers and Other Hardware" and click the left mouse button once. Another screen appears. Left-click on the "Mouse" icon. A dialog box will appear. Next, left click on the "Pointer Options" tab. Then left-click on the box next to "Display pointer trails". Click "OK" to finish. You'll notice the difference immediately.

You can also make the arrow pointer itself larger. Follow the above steps to display the mouse control panel and select the "Pointers" tab. Then click the inverted arrow next to "Windows Default" (System Scheme). Left click on one of the schemes that has "large" or "extra large" in the title. Click "OK" to finish. Don't worry – you can put either of these changes back to their original state by going back and selecting the original option. Go ahead and experiment if you'd like; you won't break anything.

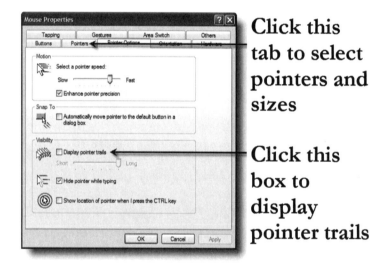

Click this tab to select pointers and sizes

Click this box to display pointer trails

Oh, and if you're one of the 10% of the population that is left-handed, the mouse control panel will allow you to reverse the buttons. For the sake of simplicity, I'll still refer to "left-clicking" and "right-clicking" based on the default, right-hand mouse setting.

TOP SECRET Here's a tip if your laptop computer has a trackpad – a recessed area you move your finger across to move the pointer. If you have intermittent trouble moving the pointer, try licking the tip of your finger. This seems to make control much easier and precise on some trackpads.

The Keyboard

A computer keyboard works much like a typewriter. Suffice to say that keys are pressed to enter text. However, there are a few "computerisms" that occasionally throw a wrench into the works of common sense.

Let's take a look at all the potential "gotchas" when dealing with this seemingly straightforward piece of equipment.

Some keyboards have a separate number entry keypad located to the right of the main keys. If this keypad doesn't work – you press the keys and nothing happens – press the "num lock" key usually located at the top left of the keypad. A small indicator light may or may not go on.[*] When entering

---

[*] I fully realize that this isn't exactly the definitive, rock-solid kind of information you may be looking for. Lack of standards and lack of following the standards that exist, make learning and teaching the PC more difficult than it should be.

numbers, you can use either the keys located along the top of the alpha keys or the keypad.

- There is no "any" key. When working on a PC you may get a message that states "Press any key to continue". Simply press any key you would like. You laugh, but many, many people have called tech support and asked "where is the any key"?

- The keys labeled "ctrl" (pronounced "control") and "alt" are used for keyboard shortcuts. Keyboard shortcuts are used to execute commands that would normally be done with the mouse. This is simply another way of performing the same task. For example, as you'll learn, clicking the red "X" box in the upper right-hand corner of a window will close the window. This same thing can be accomplished by holding down the "alt" key and pressing the "F4" key. Pulling down a menu will often show what at first glance appears to be hieroglyphics along the right side of the menu. These are in fact keyboard shortcuts. This is a reminder that these menu items can also be selected by typing the listed keys. The choice is yours.

Keyboard shortcuts listed across from menu items

TOP SECRET As you begin your PC learning journey, focus on using the mouse and keeping things simple. Don't worry about keyboard shortcuts. As your skills and knowledge increase, try to gradually incorporate these shortcuts into your everyday tasks. Keyboard shortcuts can be a big time saver as they keep both hands near the keyboard and reduce the "reaching for the mouse" time. I am not sure it's completely possible to do *everything* on a PC with only keyboard commands, but I had a friend who was a technical writer and he rarely used the mouse.

- The keys labeled "ctrl" and "alt" are also used as modifiers. Click an icon with the mouse and it becomes slightly darker, thus being "selected" or "highlighted". Click another icon, and the first icon will change back to its unselected state and the new icon will become selected. However, if before you click on the second icon you were to hold down the "ctrl" key, both icons will become selected. This is called extended selection and is extremely useful when moving files.

- Most Windows keyboards include two or three extra keys whose usage is, well, let's just say "less than obvious". After exhaustive research...alright, just trying them, I determined that the one or two keys with the Windows logo (looks like a wavy, four-panel flag ⊞) display the Start menu. The "application key", which has a menu and mouse pointer printed on it, is the equivalent of a right-click with the mouse at the current location of the cursor – this will display a context-sensitive menu if one is available. In addition, these two Windows keys can be used in combination with regular keys as keyboard shortcuts. Check Chapter 3 for a complete table of keyboard shortcuts.

- If your keyboard has "sysrq" and "scroll lock" (sometimes just labeled "scroll") keys, even the aforementioned exhaustive research won't reveal their primary function. This is because they don't have a primary function – well, on some systems pressing scroll lock will turn on a tiny light. Seriously. Both these keys are holdovers from computing days (thankfully) gone by and, as far as I can tell, provide no functionality in Windows.*

- The arrow keys do different things depending on which application is open. Pressing them in a Windows window (hmmm) causes selection to shift from one icon to the next. In most word processing applications, pressing the arrow keys moves the cursor around the text.

- There is a key labeled "Enter" located where a typewriter would normally have a key labeled "Return". On a typewriter this key moves the carriage over and down one line to continue typing when the end of a line is reached. On a computer, this is unnecessary – lines wrap automatically. Enter is used, at least when typing text, to signify the start of a new paragraph and move the cursor down one line and to the left. In most other contexts, the enter key signifies "go" or "ok" or not surprisingly, "enter".

- The "backspace" key deletes text to the left of the cursor. The "delete" key deletes text to the right of the cursor. Pressing the delete key will also delete a selected item,

* Of course there is an exception, and before I start getting e-mails let me explain. There are applications used to connect PCs to legacy systems (read: old computer dinosaurs that should have been sent to the scrap heap years ago) called "terminal emulation" programs. It's possible, perhaps even likely, that these applications could use the aforementioned keys. The scroll lock light is pretty though, don't you think?

such as a file or block of selected text.

TOP SECRET Pressing the F1 key will generally display help for the current application. If you get stuck and don't know what to do, press F1.

Try not to get too caught up in the function of every key. This is good advice in general. Learn as you need to know.

My Mom, as overwhelmed as she initially was when she got her PC, still wanted to know what every button, icon, picture, and menu item did. Once, while visiting her for a "computer lesson", I found a post-it note that said "Mike, what is middle wheel on mouse"?

TOP SECRET And to end this chapter, one last very important secret. Many times, especially when you're just starting out and learning to use your new PC, you'll do something – click on an item, or hit a key accidentally – and something bad, or at least unexpected, will happen. Perhaps you're filling out a long form on a website and you inadvertently press tab and erase a bunch of text you entered in a field box, or you accidentally delete an object in a document. You could retype everything, or re-insert the object, but there is a much easier way. Press the control key and the "z" key! This is the universal keyboard command for "undo", which erases whatever you did last. This seemingly simple command will save you many, many times. Remember, if something unexpected happens or you don't know why something happened, press "ctrl-z" to get back to where you were. If you happen to watch a seasoned PC user, you may notice their left hand twitching like a bulldog chewing a wasp. This isn't the beginning of a neurological disorder, but the preemptive reflex of the ctrl-z instinct. You'll know you're a seasoned veteran when you lock your keys in your car and instinctively reach for ctrl-z....

Chapter 3

Interacting with the PC

Windows is what is known in geektown as a GUI – Graphical User Interface. Instead of entering text commands, graphic screen objects are manipulated in various ways to accomplish tasks.

There are several advantages to a GUI. One is that there is no need to memorize text commands and specific syntax as is necessary with a command-line interface. This is a good thing as a misspelled command or misplaced period, could in some cases, have very disastrous effects!

Another advantage is the "intuitive nature" of such an interface. By design this interface should be able to be used with little instruction. Ideally, the interface should be self-teaching. To some extent this is true, and Windows has come a long way in usability and user-friendliness over the years.

Much like learning to drive a car, the specifics of using the controls can be confusing at first. Once you understand how they work though, their usage becomes second-nature.

In this chapter you will find descriptions of each type of control found in Windows and Windows applications. Also, we'll take a look at some of the more useful Windows components.

Windows

Windows are the foundation of, um, Windows. In this context I am referring to windows, un-capitalized.

Think of windows as frames, like a picture frame. These frames hold almost everything displayed on the screen, such as folders, toolbars, and work spaces. Virtually every computer activity takes place within a window.

Here are two typical windows.

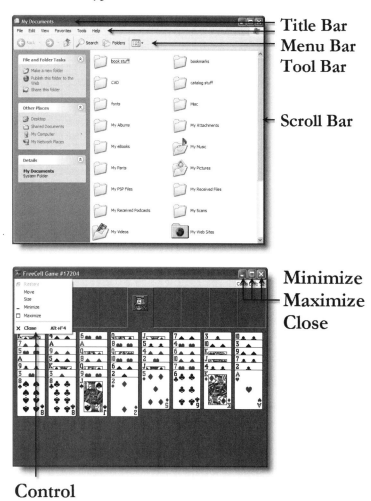

Title Bar
Menu Bar
Tool Bar

Scroll Bar

Minimize
Maximize
Close

Control
Menu

The window is really just the outside frame of the graphics above. However, it is composed of several other pieces or "controls", such as the Title Bar covered in the next section.

TOP SECRET Only one window can be active at a time. This is called "selected" or "having the focus". The window is made active by clicking anywhere within it, or by clicking its button on the Taskbar.

Title Bar

Take a look at the previous two windows. The top line is the Title Bar. Notice the title in each bar. One is "My Documents", the other "FreeCell Game #17204".

The Title Bar always contains a title. It also holds a number of other controls we will review shortly.

There are a few actions the Title Bar responds to. First, by placing the cursor over the Title Bar and holding down the left mouse button, the window can be dragged around the screen if the window is less than full-screen size. Second, double-clicking on the Title Bar will both maximize and "restore down" the window depending on its current state. "Restore down" is a Microsoft-ism for "make window smaller than full-screen".

Minimize, Maximize, Close Boxes

Located in the upper right corner of every window are three window controls; minimize, maximize, and close.

The left-most control, looks like a dash, is the minimize box. Clicking on it causes the window to collapse down on the Taskbar (described in the next section).

The middle button, maximize, (the overlapping squares) causes a window that is less than full-screen in size (but not minimized) to expand to fill the entire screen.

The "minimize" and maximize" controls are used primarily when you have several different windows on-screen. This allows you to make other windows active.

Clicking on the close box, (the "X" in the upper right corner) causes the window to completely disappear. To get it back will require you to follow whatever initial steps were required to open it in the first place.

However, if the window you're trying to close contains an unsaved file (Chapter 4), the window will not immediately disappear. Instead a warning dialog box will appear prompting you to choose whether you want to save or discard the file before closing. If you click "No" in this box, the window disappears and and the file you were working on is gone – forever. Clicking "Yes" brings up a standard file dialog box prompting you to select a location and name for your file. Clicking on "Cancel", cancels your request to close or exit the window and leaves it open. Note that clicking on the close box located on the warning dialog box is the same as clicking on "cancel".

58

Also note the "Control Menu" in the previous window graphic. This menu, accessed by left-clicking the icon located in the upper left corner of a window, contains redundant controls. That is, all of these menu items can be accomplished by other means. This menu simply offers convenience if, for example, only the upper left corner of a window is visible.

TOP SECRET While most menus require the user to click once to display the menu and then scroll down and click again on the menu item, you can quickly select the "Close" menu item from the Control Menu by double-clicking on the Control Menu icon. This can come in very hand as it allows you to close a window from either side of the screen. Mousing from one side to the other can get tiresome....

Taskbar

The Taskbar, by default at least, is located on the bottom of the Desktop screen. It's easily identifiable by the Windows logo and the word "Start" located on the left.

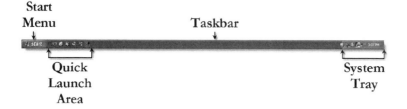

The Taskbar serves many functions and is comprised of four separate parts; Start menu, Quick Launch area, Taskbar, and System Tray, also called the Notification Area.

TOP SECRET The Taskbar by default appears on the bottom of the Desktop. However, you can move the whole thing, Start menu and all, to either side or even the top of the Desktop. Right-click any empty space on the Taskbar and verify that there is no check mark next to "Lock the Taskbar". Then click and drag the Taskbar to any side or top of the Desktop. The graphic below shows the Taskbar moved to the right side of the Desktop.

Taskbar moved to right side of Desktop. Note Start menu button on top of screen

The Start menu itself is a main feature in Windows. In fact, some research suggests that for many users, the Start menu is the primary method of interacting with Windows. Oddly, Microsoft has chosen not to capitalize the word "start" when used to identify the Start menu. I've chosen to capitalize it to avoid confusion.

60

The Start menu, far from being an "as-is" device, is highly configurable and can be used as a quick way to access frequently used programs.

To display the Start menu, click once on the word "Start". To select a menu item, click once on the item. Right pointing arrows indicate that a sub-menu exists. To display the sub-menu, hold the mouse still over the menu item that has an arrow for just a second – the sub-menu is displayed.

The Start menu is comprised of four sections:

● **Pinned Items** – This section is for your most frequently used applications and documents. To change items here, simply click and drag them to or from. Once icons are in the pinned area, you can change the order they appear by again clicking and dragging.

● **Most Often Used Items Area** – This area is not user-configurable. This is where Windows makes educated guesses, based on your personal computing habits, as to what will go in this area. Oddly, it seems to constantly put Microsoft programs in this area even though I rarely use them.... You can't add items to this area manually, but you can delete them if you want by either right-click→Remove from This List, or by clicking and dragging them off the list.

● **Windows Components** – This area holds icons linked to frequently used areas of Windows. While this area is not completely user-configurable, there are several properties that control what is displayed in this area. Accessing these properties is described below.

● **Master List of Applications** – A user-configurable menu of virtually every piece of usable software on a PC. Most application installers place "shortcuts" to applications on this menu or at least give you the option of doing so.* In addition, users are free to add, delete, or re-organize this menu as needed by dragging and dropping, using the right-click context menu, or by using Explorer outlined in Chapter 4.

Aside from dragging/dropping and deleting, Start menu properties can also be changed by right-clicking on the word "Start" and selecting "Properties". Many options are available. For now, just be aware of the location of these options.

---

* "Shortcuts" are simply files that contain nothing but directions to other files. This allows you to place icons for an application in several different areas, such as the Start menu, the Desktop, and the Quicklaunch bar, all without duplicating the actual application.

The Quick Launch bar is located immediately to the right of the Start menu. It is an area that holds icons of your most frequently used programs. Although icons probably already exist in your Quick Launch bar, you can customize it to your needs.

Quick
Launch area

The Quick Launch bar is delineated by two vertical rows of dots – if the Taskbar is not locked. Any changes made to the Taskbar require it to be unlocked. To unlock the Taskbar, right-click anywhere on it and select "Lock the Taskbar" from the context menu.

TOP SECRET No Quick Launch area on your Taskbar? Whether or not the Quick Launch area is visible depends on a specific setting. Depending on who originally installed your version of Windows, it may or may not be visible. To turn on or off Quick Launch, right-click on the Taskbar and select properties.

Click this box to turn on Quick Launch area

Any icon can be dragged to the Quick Launch area. Also, the order the icons are arranged can be changed by dragging them anywhere on the bar you wish. In the bar above I have six icons; five for frequently used applications and the "Show Desktop" icon, which is second from the left. Clicking on the this icon minimizes all windows and shows the Desktop.

The Taskbar area is defined on the left by the Quick Launch bar, and on the right by the left-pointing arrow. The Taskbar displays open windows and allows you to easily switch which window is active (selected) just by clicking on the Taskbar button.

The Taskbar above shows four open windows; a word processor, two FireFox browser windows and the FreeCell card game. Note that the FreeCell window is currently the active window as indicated by its darker color. Remember, only one window at a time can be active.

To make another window active, click on its name in the Taskbar.

The last area on the Taskbar, the System Tray, displays icons of commonly used utilities and programs that load automatically when the computer starts-up. It also displays the time and, if you hold the mouse over the time, the date.

Generally, the items located in the System Tray are "set and forget". Once they are configured to your liking, you rarely have to fool around with them.

Configuring individual items located in the System Tray is accomplished either by double-clicking the icon or right-clicking on it. Both ways are usually equivalent.

The System Tray has built-in intelligence. (Ha!) It remembers which icons you frequently access and hides the rest. You can expand or contract the System Tray by clicking the arrow located on the left. Expanding the tray displays all the items located there. Also note that hovering the cursor over a System Tray icon displays a text box (tooltip) describing the application. You can also override the built-in "intelligence" and manually control what items appear in the System Tray by right-clicking in an empty area, selecting "Properties", and clicking the "Customize" button.

Oh, one other thing, even though the System Tray has existed for years in various versions of Windows, apparently Microsoft decided to rename it to "Notification Area" for Windows XP. I have no idea why – I doubt they do either.

Amazingly, doing a search on "system tray" (Start→Help and Support→Search), displays only topics on "Notification Area", so I guess they're serious about the change....

Scroll Bars

Scroll bars are usually located on the right and bottom sides of most windows. They consist of arrows at each end and a bar, sometimes called the "elevator" or "thumb", that slides back and forth between the arrows and determines what is visible within the window.

Scroll bars are fairly intuitive to use. Try them and you'll get the general idea, though here are a few things you might not figure out too quickly:

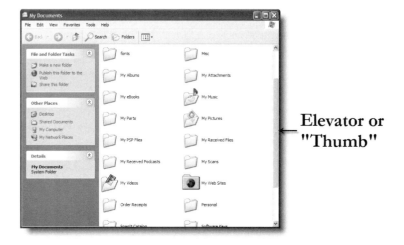

Elevator or "Thumb"

- You can scroll a document by clicking on the arrows located at each end of the scroll bar. This gives a fine scrolling action.

- You can also scroll by clicking the blank areas above and below the elevator bar. This usually moves the document one viewable page.

- You can scroll by grabbing the elevator bar (left click and hold down) and moving it wherever you need to.

- The size of the the "thumb" or "elevator" is relative to the size of the entire document. Large documents, which means that only a small percentage of the total document is viewable at any one time, have very small elevator bars.

- Scroll bars appear and disappear automatically as needed when a window is resized. If the entire contents of a window are displayed, there will be no scrollbar.

Dialog Boxes

Dialog boxes are not technically controls. Instead, they are a type of specialized window that hold various controls.

Below are two examples of dialog boxes.

Dialog boxes are displayed when software needs information from you to continue, hence the name "dialog" – the PC needs to have a conversation with you. The computer is asking you to input information. The next six controls are usually, but not always, contained within a dialog box.

List Boxes

List boxes are used when there are multiple choices. They can be found on toolbars or in dialog boxes.

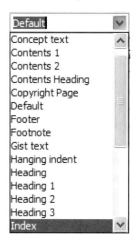

To use, click on the arrow. A drop down list of options is displayed. Click once on the option you desire. If more options exist than can be displayed at one time, a scroll bar will appear on the side of the list. Use it to scroll up or down, then click on the desired selection.

Radio Buttons

Radio buttons also offer multiple choices. Generally, only one can be selected at a time. Usage is very easy, click on the selection you desire and click the "OK" button.

Note that selecting the last radio button (Variable) will enable the list box in the above example.

Check Boxes

Check boxes are similar to radio buttons – a simple click selects them. The main difference is that check boxes present a list of multiple choices where more than one may be selected at a time. Note that you must click the "OK" button for any of your check boxes to take effect. This also applies to radio buttons as just discussed.

Buttons

Buttons are very easy to figure out. They do one thing and that one thing is printed right on them. In the above graphic, you'll see the "OK", "Cancel", and "Customize" buttons. A single click activates the button.

Most dialog boxes contain "OK" and "Cancel" buttons. Clicking "OK" will implement any changes you've made using the controls contained within the dialog box. Clicking "Cancel" will negate any changes you've made using the controls contained within the dialog box. Put another way for clarification: if you change settings and then click the "Cancel" button, your changes will *not* take effect. Important to remember....

TOP SECRET **Buttons can also be activated without using the mouse. Take another look at the buttons in the graphic above. Notice that the "OK" button has a darker line around it? That button is selected. Pressing the "Enter" key will activate the button just the same as clicking the mouse on it. When a dialog box is displayed, the most logical button (at least according to the software designer) will be selected by default. To select other buttons, press the tab key repeatedly to cycle though all available buttons.**

Field Boxes

Field boxes, often called "fields", are boxes that take information. They are used in a variety of places from preferences in applications to forms on websites. Usually, one field is selected by default and contains a blinking text cursor so you can just start typing. If a text cursor does not appear in any field, click once in the field you wish to fill out. Once a field box is selected, pressing the tab key will select other field boxes allowing you to fill out all the fields without removing your hands from the keyboard.

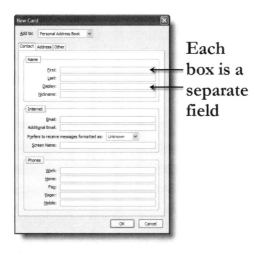

Each box is a separate field

Arrow Scrollers

Arrow scrollers are a window control used to select a value. They consist of at least two parts, the display (or field), which contains the value(s), and the arrows, used to change the value(s).

The following dialog box contains two arrow scroller controls, the year (containing 2005), and the time (containing 10:41:37 AM). The control containing the month of February is a drop-down list box.

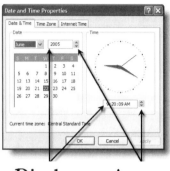

Displays   Arrows

To use the arrow scroller control, click on the arrows to either increase or decrease the value in the display box. Some arrow scrollers have multiple fields in the display area. In the above example, the time display actually contains four separate fields; hour, minute, seconds, and AM/PM. To change the value of a specific field, click on it in the display area, it becomes highlighted (selected). Then click on the arrows to change the value. You can select additional fields by pressing the tab key.

Sliders

Slider controls work similarly to the light dimmer switches you might have in your home. That is, they vary the intensity of whatever they control.

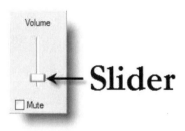

72

To use sliders, just grab (hold down left mouse button) and drag the slider to whatever position you want.

Volume control is the most frequently encountered slider.

Toolbars

Toolbars are used in almost all applications. Essentially, a toolbar is nothing more than a string of buttons linked together. An icon on each button depicts the purpose of each specific tool and is selected by clicking on it. Tools are generally of the toggle type – that is, they are selected unless they are clicked again or another tool is selected.

 Toolbars

With many toolbars, the icons depicting each tool are woefully inadequate in conveying the purpose of the tool. To get a text summary of each tool, hover the cursor over the tool icon and a "tooltip" will appear with the name of the tool. Not always very descriptive, but better than the icon.

Tooltip

Hyperlinks

A hyperlink is a portion of text, or graphic, that works like an icon – clicking on it initiates an action. That action may be linked to anything in an application, such as a tool or dialog box.

Prior to the release of Windows XP, hyperlinks were mainly used in web pages,. Clicking on a hyperlink located on a web page causes another page or portion of a page to be displayed. Hyperlinks are the main navigational tool of the Internet.

Hyperlinks, often called "links", are identified by words or phrases appearing in different colors (though almost always medium blue) and sometimes underlined. Graphics, usually with a medium blue border, can also be hyperlinks.

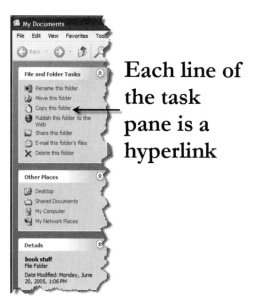

Each line of the task pane is a hyperlink

Hyperlinks can also be identified by the mouse cursor. Hovering the cursor over a hyperlink will cause the cursor to change to a hand with forefinger extended.

In the example below, I've placed the mouse pointer over a hyperlink. This causes the pointer to change to a hand with outstretched finger and display a tooltip.

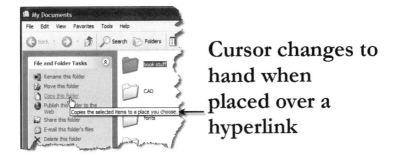

Cursor changes to hand when placed over a hyperlink

Menus

This section has nothing to do with restaurants, but software menus are similar to food menus. Both are lists that the diner, or in this case, user, choose from.

On a PC this is done by clicking once on the menu name, then moving the mouse up or down to highlight the menu selection you desire and clicking again.

Some standardization of menus does exist in Windows software. Most applications have a "File", "Edit", and "Help" menu. The menu items contained within these menus are generally the same, but vary depending on the specific program. See Chapter 5 for more details.

Click once on menu name to display menu items

As previously discussed in Chapter 2, The Mouse and Keyboard, context-sensitive menus are displayed by right-clicking on an object. When in doubt, right-click! You'll find access to many often-used commands by right-clicking on objects.

Keyboard Shortcuts

I have a love/hate relationship with keyboard shortcuts. I love them because I can keep both hands on the keyboard and don't have to keep groping for the mouse. I hate them because I can rarely, if ever, remember them. Sure, I could take the time and really learn them, but I guess I am lazy and never have. But I have memorized a handful of the most commonly used commands and recommend you do as well.

Keyboard shortcuts are a way of initiating an action without using the mouse; only keys are used, hence the name. Hold down the first key, and press the second key once to perform a keyboard shortcut. Keyboard shortcuts vary from other window controls in that their usage is totally optional – they exist as an alternate way to accomplish tasks normally done with the mouse.

Several standard (meaning universal to all programs and Windows itself) keyboard shortcuts exist. As you become more familiar with your PC, you may wish to try them. Particularly useful are the first five; copy, cut, paste, undo, and close active window.

Press	To
ctrl+c	Copy
ctrl+x	Cut
ctrl+v	Paste
ctrl+z	Undo
alt+f4	Close the active item, or quit the active program.
ctrl+f4	Close the active document in programs that allow you to have multiple documents open simultaneously.
alt+tab	Switch between open items.
shift+delete	Delete selected item permanently without placing the item in the Recycle Bin.

Press	To
ctrl while dragging an item	Copy selected item
ctrl+shift while dragging an item	Create shortcut to selected item.
f2	Rename selected item.
ctrl+right arrow	Move the insertion point to the beginning of the next word.
ctrl+left arrow	Move the insertion point to the beginning of the previous word.
ctrl+down arrow	Move the insertion point to the beginning of the next paragraph.
ctrl+up arrow	Move the insertion point to the beginning of the previous paragraph.
ctrl+shift with any of the arrow keys	Highlight a block of text
Shift with any of the arrow keys	Select more than one item in a window or on the Desktop, or select text within a document.

Press	To
f3	Search for a file or folder.
alt+enter	View properties for the selected item.
alt+enter	Displays the properties of the selected object.
alt+spacebar	Opens the shortcut menu for the active window.
alt+esc	Cycle through items in the order they were opened.
f6	Cycle through screen elements in a window or on the Desktop.
shift+f10	Display the shortcut menu for the selected item.
alt+spacebar	Display the System menu for the active window.
ctrl+esc	Display the **Start menu**.
alt+Underlined letter in menu name	Display the corresponding menu.

Press	To
Underlined letter in a command name on an open menu	Carry out the corresponding command.
f10	Activate the menu bar in the active program.
right arrow	Open the next menu to the right, or open a submenu.
left arrow	Open the next menu to the left, or close a submenu.
f5	Refresh the active window.
Backspace	View the folder one level up in "My Computer" or Windows Explorer.
esc	Cancel the current task.
Shift when you insert a CD into the CD-ROM drive	Prevent the CD from automatically playing.
ctrl+tab	Move forward through tabs.
ctrl+shift+tab	Move backward through tabs.

Press	To
tab	Move forward through options.
shift+tab	Move backward through options.
alt+underlined letter	Carry out the corresponding command or select the corresponding option.
enter	Carry out the command for the active option or button.
spacebar	Select or clear the check box if the active option is a check box.
arrow keys	Select a button if the active option is a group of option buttons.
f1	Display Help.
backspace	Opens a folder one level up if a folder is selected in the **Save As** or **Open** dialog box.

The Windows logo ⊞ key, if your keyboard has it, offers a few useful keyboard shortcuts.

Press	To
Windows key (⊞) + d	Hides or shows all application windows or Desktop.
Windows key (⊞) + e	Opens "My Computer" in Windows Explorer.
Windows key (⊞) + f	Opens the search window.
Windows key(⊞) + r	Opens the Run command.

Many applications offer keyboard shortcuts for some or all menu commands. Helpfully, they are printed across from the actual menu commands as reminders. When selecting a menu command, take a glance at the shortcut reminders for next time.

Keyboard shortcuts

In the graphic you'll note that pressing "ctrl-v" pastes into the current document and is the equivalent of selecting "Paste" from that menu.

Wizards

Wizards (no magic wands, no pointy hats) are Microsoft's newest attempt at "simplifying" Windows. Wizards, in this context, refer to applications (or part of an application) that hold your hand through specific tasks. For example, the Windows OS has dozens of wizards for such tasks as adding hardware, e-mailing pictures, setting up Internet connections, and creating user accounts.

Some users have referred to Wizards as "interviews". You are typically asked a series of questions until the Wizard has enough information to complete whatever task you've requested.

You'll find wizards abound in Windows XP and newly released applications. The most ridiculous usage of this is XP's "Desktop Cleanup Wizard". It seems that too many PC users are cluttering up their Desktop with icons *and* are incapable of dragging unused shortcuts to the trash on their own.* The Desktop Cleanup Wizard, which is run on some systems automatically every 60 days, walks the user through the task of placing unused icons in a "unused Desktop shortcuts" folder located....wait for it.....on the Desktop. Sigh.

Sorry about the rambling....

---

* While creating and placing shortcuts for commonly used items on the Desktop does increase convenience, it also increases memory (RAM) usage. Try to keep the Desktop as clear and uncluttered as possible. My personal Desktop has only the Recycle Bin, a temporary folder (where I store downloads), and a document or two.

Anyway, most wizards appear something like the next four graphics.

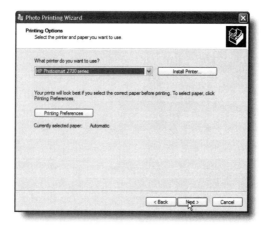

As you can see, wizards are really just a series of dialog boxes. Provide the needed information and click the "Next" button to continue through the wizard. Also note that generally, but not always, there is an alternate way to accomplish wizard tasks without using the wizard.

Expand and Contract Controls

Expand and Contract controls can be thought of as "show and hide" controls. They control how much information is shown at any one time. For example, Windows Explorer uses these controls to display and hide specific folders and files. Most of the time these controls are in the form of "+" and "-" signs. Clicking "+" expands the listing and clicking "-" contracts or collapses the list into headings or sections.

Expand and contract controls used to show and hide files in Windows Explorer

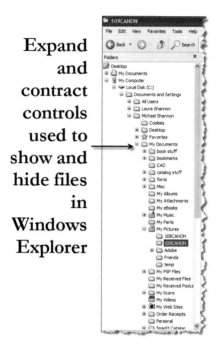

With the release of Windows XP, you'll also find up and down arrows for expand and contract as seen below:

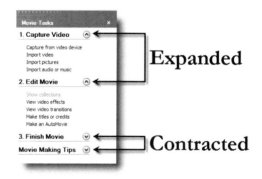

Expanded

Contracted

In the example above, the headings are the lines with the arrows located on the right side. In this case the top two headings are expanded and the bottom two are contracted*. Note the down arrow indicating this.

On occasion you might run into left and right facing arrows that expand/contract. The only example I've run across though, is the arrow to show/hide the System Tray icons.

Forward and Back Arrows

Forward and back arrows are fairly self-explanatory. In addition, this material is covered in-depth in Chapter 4, Navigation and Files. But let's briefly examine them here, as these controls are found in a number of areas. These type of navigation arrows are used in web browsers, Windows Explorer, as well as other applications.

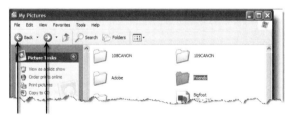

Clicking these controls moves
you forward or back

---

* This screen shot is from Windows Movie Maker. This is an application you can use to edit movies taken with your camcorder. If your computer came with Windows XP service pack 2 pre-installed, you probably already have this application installed. Check the Start menu. Also see Chapter 12 to find out how to tell what version of Windows you have.

There are two main concepts to remember when using these arrows. First, you should remember where you originally started from, called "home". Second, the arrows will be ghosted (greyed-out) and useless unless you've already gone backwards or forwards. So these controls are mainly convenience features.

Tooltips

Tooltips are not really a control per se, and I have mentioned them before, but best to be thorough. Tooltips are the small text box that appears near the cursor when the cursor is hovered over an object. The object can be anything from a window control, to icons in the System Tray. When you have a question about what something is, try hovering the cursor over the item. The graphic below shows the tooltip displayed when the cursor is hovered over the drop-down zoom control of Microsoft Works.

Movie /VCR Controller

When PCs first became popular there were only a few things you could use them for. Most early PCs were used for word processing, desktop publishing, number crunching (spreadsheets) and of course, games.

Today, PCs are bought to accomplish dozens of tasks, many

of which can be done no other way. Certainly, getting on the Internet is the most common usage of a PC.

Increasingly though, people are taking advantage of the multimedia capabilities of the PC. This includes creating and viewing video and music files.

The movie controller is found in most applications that create or play video and sound files. It's simple to use and directly analogous to the controls used on VCRs, DVD players, and CD players that you probably have around your home. The screen shot below shows the movie controls from Microsoft Movie Maker.

The controls from left to right are: play, stop, rewind, frame back, frame forward, and fast forward. The last two buttons on the right are not part of the movie control.

Different applications might use slightly different controls. For example, a music application might omit the frame forward/frame back controls entirely or substitute other functions. Hovering the cursor over the individual buttons will display a tooltip containing the buttons function.

TOP SECRET **Controls used to interact with software are designed to be intuitive. That is, little or no explanation is required to operate them. Generally this is true, after even minimal time spent experimenting.**

So, go ahead and experiment! It's unlikely you'll break anything and nothing will help you more than real experience. Remember, if you are unsure of what something does, try hovering the mouse cursor over the item to display a tooltip.

Windows Components

There are a few "pieces" of Windows that are integral to its operation. The pieces, or components, as I'll refer to them from here on out, are really just icons representing files (see next chapter). But these particular icons represent important utilities and tools that you will find useful.

My Computer

The "My Computer" icon is really the front door to a PC – behind it is everything contained on your computer. All the hardware and all the software can be accessed through the "My Computer" icon.

So, just where is the "My Computer" icon? Well, it depends on your computer and the way XP was installed and configured.

In past versions of Windows, "My Computer" was located on the Desktop. You booted up the PC and there it was, waiting for you to double-click on it.

With XP, it may be on the Desktop – or it may not. Same goes for finding it in the Start menu – maybe, maybe not. There are now settings to determine where the "My Computer" icon is displayed.

If "My Computer" is not on your Desktop or on your Start menu, you can make it appear in the following way:

To Make "My Computer" appear on your Desktop:

1. Right-click anywhere on the Desktop and select "Properties".

2. Click the "Customize Desktop" button.

3. Make sure the "Desktop" tab is selected at the top of the dialog box.

Click the "My Computer" box, then click the "OK" button to display the "My Computer icon on your Desktop

4. Click the "My Computer" check box and then the OK button.

To make "My Computer" appear on the Start menu:

1. Right-click on the word "Start".

2. Select "Properties".

3. Make sure the "Start menu" tab is selected.

4. Click the "Customize" button.

5. Click on the "Advanced" tab.

6. Click the radio button "Display as a link" under "My Computer".

7. Click the "OK" button.

Now that you can see the "My Computer" icon, what do you do with it? Again, all hardware and software can be accessed by double-clicking this icon. And though there are several other ways to access hardware and software, "My Computer" holds it all in one place. So if you need to access something, this is an excellent place to start. Just double-click it like any other icon to get started. While you may not need to access this area now, you should at least know how to find it.

Task Pane

The Task Pane is a new addition to Windows XP and appears on the left side of every Desktop window, including the "My Computer" window described above. Desktop windows, sometimes called Explorer windows, are displayed whenever you double-click or select from the Start menu:

- A folder

- A storage device, such as a hard disk or CD-ROM

- The "My Computer" icon.

Taskpane

Essentially, Microsoft has added commands to this area that previously were found only by right-clicking on objects. But as hardly anyone was right-clicking on anything, we now have the Task Pane.

Clicking on the text commands in the Task Pane area causes them to be run. These commands change in relation to the object selected in the right pane or main Explorer window. So, like the right-click menu, Task Pane commands are "context-sensitive".

Note the expand and contract arrow control located on the Task Pane. Use these to see or hide additional commands and information.

Arrow controls show/hide commands

Commands change based on what object is selected in right pane

Details area shows information on selected object

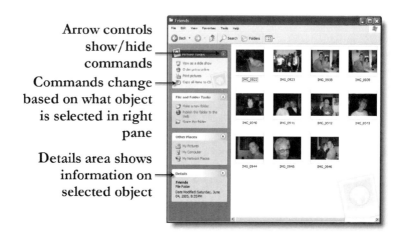

Also note the "Details" area. By expanding this area and selecting a file, detailed and useful information will be displayed.

These Explorer windows are very useful for finding and accessing files. For example, perhaps you're looking for a specific photo that is located logically enough in the "My Pictures" folder. A good way to browse this folder is to select "My Pictures" from the Start menu. But what if you decide that the item you're looking for is located in a completely different folder? You could use the "Up" button on the toolbar to navigate up through various folders. However, Desktop windows offer a secret function – clicking the "Folders" button on the toolbar displays an overview "map" of everything on your PC! This allows you to see all the folders at once and select the one you need.

In the past, this map or view was available only by explicitly starting the Explorer program. Now you can get this view in any Desktop window simply by clicking the "Folders" icon. This is an important concept and will be discussed in detail in the next chapter.

**Folders
Button**

**Task pane
area changes
to Explorer
view**

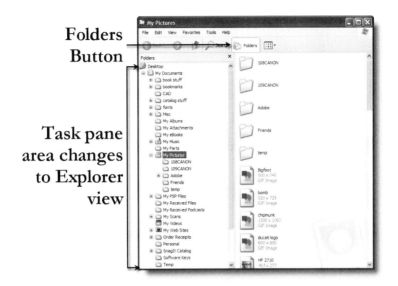

Control Panels

Control panels are icons representing applications that control the behavior and appearance of the Windows operating system. There are tens of thousands of options held within the recesses of all the control panels and you could spend days exploring them all – and, I encourage you to do so. Explore that is, not spend days doing it....

The control panel applications use standard Windows controls described throughout to configure properties and settings to your taste.

While these settings can make Windows easier to use in some cases, you don't have to change anything to begin using your PC. Changing control panel settings is completely optional.

Select this menu item to display control panels

To get to the Control Panels, **Start→Control Panel.**

Accounts

Accounts provide the solution to a couple of dilemmas:

- Privacy – How do you prevent other users of your PC from seeing all your stuff? Think "private" picture collections or personal financial data.

- Stability – How to prevent others users, such as children and complete novices, from screwing up the computer so it no longer works?

- Security – How do you prevent unauthorized people from using your PC at all?

Accounts solve all of these problems. If your PC will be used by multiple users, each person should ideally have a separate account. When they use the computer, they will enter their unique username and password.

Each account has separate areas for storing files and settings, so each user will only have access to their own stuff. In addition, any customizations such as Desktop pictures and mouse settings, will appear for each specific user. So, if your kids decide to replace your beautiful mountain landscape Desktop wallpaper with the logo from the Insane Clown Posse, at least you won't have to look at it.

When you initially booted up your PC you were asked for a name and a password. This created the first account – an account with important special privileges called the "Administrator" account. This account makes you God of your PC world. Only an administrator account can install software, make certain changes in Control Panels, create and edit accounts, and see and manipulate every file on your PC. Multiple administrator accounts can exist, though you're asking for trouble if you bestow these powers on more than one user. I recommend having only one account with administrator privileges.

Most users should be given "Limited" accounts. While these accounts are limited compared to Administrator accounts, they provide all the features and usability a person would need for a happy computing life. In fact, since Limited account users can only view their own files, certain views and tasks are simplified.

Aside from the initial account created when you first booted your new PC, if other people are going to be using the PC, give them each their own account.

To add accounts for additional users, go to Start→Control Panel and click on "User Accounts".

Click here to add accounts for additional users of your PC

What if you want each user to have their own Windows customizations but still want the ability to see each others' files? By default, Windows creates a "Shared Documents" folder accessible by opening "My Computer". This folder is also accessed through Explorer and file save/open dialog boxes. Files placed in this location are usable by anyone with an account. Account owners will still not be able to view other users files placed in their own respective "My Documents" folders.

Chapter 4

Navigation and Files

This chapter contains the most important information in this book! Get this right and not only will you easily be able to use a PC, you'll also know more than a good majority of PC users! Seriously, take your time here and you'll reap the rewards in the end. I highly encourage you to grab your favorite beverage, sit down at your computer, and follow along with the explanations and particularly the tutorials.

These two topics are very straightforward to understand and once you have that understanding, you'll realize just how simple they really are. Unfortunately, most people never take the few minutes required to really understand these concepts and as a result, struggle to use computers.

These topics are intertwined, though you need not know one to understand the other. If you're having trouble "getting it", read through the entire chapter anyway. You may find at the end you get the "big picture"; the "AAHaa!" moment.

Navigation

So, you're on the edge of your seat patiently waiting for one of the biggest secrets in computer usage to be revealed. Ready? Here it is:

TOP SECRET Using a PC is really all about files – opening them and saving them. If you learn the structure of the Windows file system, you will find using a computer almost easy!

Really. It seems trivially easy, and it is, but many, many people using PCs are confused and annoyed by this very concept.

Consider a huge maple tree in the woods. In the ground is the base of the tree, its starting point. If someone said to you, "go to the base of a tree", assuming you don't mind some digging, you'd go to the roots. You could dig lower than the roots, but technically you're no longer having anything to do with the tree. The roots are the tree's starting point. Like a tree, when you navigate around the PC, you will always have a starting point, a base or root. This is the point from which you cannot go beyond. I know, you're saying to yourself, "What the hell is he talking about"? Hang in there with me, this will all become clear in a moment.

This is one of those "chicken and the egg" dilemmas, whereas it's extremely difficult to understand PC navigation when you've never used a PC.

Files, File systems, and Russian Nesting Dolls

As you've previously learned, everything stored on a computer, be it on the hard disk, compact disk or any other storage media is a file. Files are stored on such media in a very specific organizational structure or pattern. This structure is known as "hierarchical" and is seen in various places when using a PC.

Hierarchical is another one of "those" computer words. Sounds impressive and complicated, but really isn't. Don't let this word put you off! As you'll soon see this is very easy to visualize. In fact, it is nothing more complicated than the structure of a tree!

Ever see a set of Russian nesting dolls? You probably have. There is a big doll, usually shaped like a bowling pin. Inside are smaller dolls, each inside of one another. These dolls represent a hierarchical structure.

If you aren't familiar with these dolls, another example of a hierarchical structure that is very similar to that used on the PC, is a file cabinet. In fact, years ago when PCs were something of a novelty the "file cabinet" analogy was bandied about quite commonly to help the "newbies" learn.* I want to say it originated with Apple, but I am not quite sure. And even if I was sure, someone from Microsoft would probably contact me and tell me they came up with it first. Whatever. Today, you rarely hear or read about it. Makes too much sense me thinks, and smacks of "geek elitism".*

As a quick aside, with Windows XP, Microsoft has gone out of its way to disguise the file cabinet analogy. It is still there if you know where to look. You'll find out in the very next section titled, Explorer. In its place though, is the Taskpane with hyperlinks to commands such as "Copy this file" or "Rename this file". Sounds good at first blush, but it's kind of like getting into your car and pushing one button to go to the grocery store and another to go to the health club. Works great if that is exactly where you want to go. However, should you want to go somewhere else, or go the health club and then the grocery store, you're screwed as you don't actually know how to drive there. Stepping off the soapbox now....

* "Newbies" being an affectionate term for those not yet technologically savvy.

* Particularly prevalent in days gone by, but still occasionally raising its ugly head, "geek elitism" is a term used to describe those "in the know" and their unwillingness to share their knowledge with others of less experience. Keeps the job applicant pool small and the salaries high, ya know?

Let's envision a common two-drawer filing cabinet. You may even have one in your home or office. *A computer hard disk, usually labeled "Local Disk (C:)", is just like a file cabinet! And while you're beginning to learn to use a PC, you should actively think of your hard drive in this way.*

Inside a file cabinet are folders. Each folder may contain files, or other folders. The same holds true for a PC. The "hard disk" is the cabinet. Folders are just containers that hold other folders or files. But if everything is a file, why am I calling them "folder or files"? Folders are indeed files. Special files that are containers for other files. To simplify the concept I'll refer to folders by name.

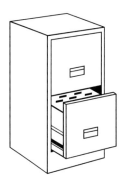

For example, imagine a file cabinet with two folders. The first folder, labeled "Paycheck Stubs", has twelve paycheck stubs, each of which is really a file. The second folder, labeled "Receipts", contains twelve other folders. Each one is labeled with one of the twelve months. Inside each month's folder are additional folders for groceries, household, car repairs, and medical. And inside each of those folders are actual receipts – files.

Understanding this hierarchical structure is very important when it comes to organizing your files, finding files, and specifically when it comes to dealing with files **you** create and save – documents. Seriously, the number one problem new computer users have is saving a file and having no idea how to find out where it is saved or how to find it.

The hierarchical structure's main claim to fame is a logical pattern of organization. This makes it easy to find and save items – if you understand the basic structure.

By studying the graphic below, you'll begin to get the gist of how this structure works.

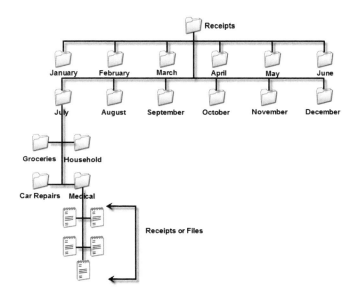

Keep in mind the following:

● When discussing this type of hierarchical structure, the base point, called "root" or "home", is at the top of the tree. In the graphic, the "Receipts" folder would be root. However, the ultimate root on a PC is the "My

Computer" icon that contains all attached storage devices.

● Most user confusion comes from not understanding why they can't "see" or find a file or folder. By studying the graphic you'll see the very simple reason for this. Obviously, if you are looking at the contents of "August/Groceries", you cannot see what is inside "April/Household". In order to see inside "April/Household", you have to navigate up to "April" and then down to "Household."

● This structure and your ability to visualize it comes into play when you're saving and opening files inside an application, while using Explorer, and to some extent, while surfing the web.

So, let's back up a moment and chat about saving files. To do this, we'll use an application installed on every Windows PC called "Notepad". Notepad is a very basic word processor. "Document" has now become a generic term for a data file – a file created by an application. All files that you personally create and save will be data files. I'll use the generic term "document" to describe these even though they may not contain text.

This tutorial will teach you the basics of saving and opening data files. Please sit down at your computer and follow along.

To start Notepad:

1. Click on the Start menu located in the left lower corner of the screen.

2. Hold the cursor over the "All Programs" area.

3. Move the mouse over to the "Accessories" folder.

4. Move the mouse over and down to "Notepad".

5. Click once on "Notepad".

Notepad will then open and look like this:

Take a look at the Title Bar and note that the current name of the document is "Untitled". This is because the document has not been saved yet. Though it is possible to save a file with the name of "Untitled" don't ever do it!

Now, lets create a simple document:

6. Make sure Notepad is the selected or active application – this should be the case unless you've inadvertently clicked outside the Notepad window. To make sure, click anywhere inside the Notepad window or by clicking the "Untitled-Notepad" button on the Taskbar.

7. Note the blinking text cursor in the upper left hand

corner of the notepad window. This indicates that the window is selected and you can begin typing.

8. Type the following sentence: The quick brown fox jumps over the lazy dog.*

Now, notepad looks like this:

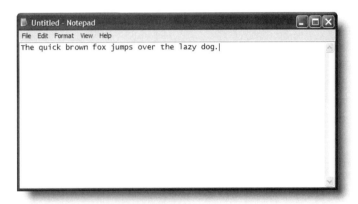

There you go! You have created your first document. Now, we need to save the document. Saving is exactly what it sounds like; saving a file to disk so you can retrieve and use it later. You wouldn't want to create a long document or a complex picture and then have it all go away, would you? *If you don't save your work, it all goes away — forever.* Save early, save often, and always save before you close the application.

To save the document:

---

* You may remember this particular sentence from typing class as it has a "special purpose", as Steve Martin might say. It contains every letter in the alphabet. Here's some more useless trivia: The longest word you can type with one hand (standard typing) is "stewardesses".

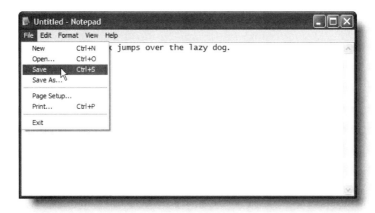

9. Click once on the "File" menu located near the top left corner of the Notepad window.

10. Move the mouse down until "Save" is highlighted.

11. Click once on "Save".

12. The Save file dialog box will open. This is how the application asks you "Hey, where would you like to save this file and what would you like to name it?"

Note that the folders displayed in your dialog box will be slightly different from mine.

When saving a file, there are a few things you need to tell the computer. First, you need to pick the location where the file will be saved. This could be anywhere you want, though for easy navigation and organization, you want to pick a spot that makes sense. You wouldn't, for example, want to place letters to friends in a folder titled "financial records" or important family photos in a folder titled "stuff". Second, you need to provide a name for the file. Again, you can name it anything you want, but try something that is readily identifiable and meaningful. Obviously a file named "Christmas letter to mom" is much more meaningful than "letter1". Then, depending on the application, you may select different file types or options. In this case we'll stick with the defaults.

Note that we are currently looking inside the "My Documents" folder as indicated in the "Save In" field. The "Save In" field always indicates the folder that is currently selected. In most cases, the folder selected for the "Save In" field is "My Documents". Sometimes however, applications will remember the last folder used and automatically open to that. None of this really matters, as you're free to navigate to wherever you wish. For the purposes of this tutorial, make sure "My Documents" appears in the "Save In" field. If not, click the "My Documents" button located on the left side of the dialog box.

TOP SECRET Generally when you save a file you will only be concerned with two things: The location where you're saving the file and the name of the file. Rarely will you have to change anything else, such as "file type". So, whenever you are presented with a save file dialog box, mentally say to yourself, "What location is appropriate for this file?" and "What is a meaningful name for this file?".

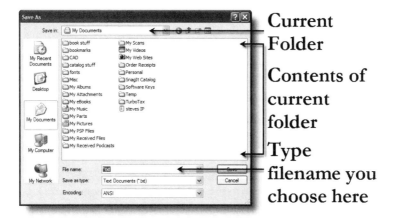

Current Folder

Contents of current folder

Type filename you choose here

13. At this point the "File Name" field contains "*.txt". This text is highlighted indicating that you can begin typing immediately. In case you're curious, the "*" is a wildcard character essentially asking you to input a name for the file. The ".txt" is just the file type that will be appended on to the file name you choose.

14. Type "my first document" and click once on the "Save" button. The dialog box disappears and the Title Bar of the Notepad application changes to the file name you just entered. You can enter any name you choose for files, but for this tutorial just go with "my first document".

You've just created and saved your first document! Congratulations!

As I'm sure you'll agree, that was relatively painless and straightforward, so let's continue.

Most of the time you'll start an application, begin creating a document, save it, work on it some more, save it, and repeat the process until the document is finished.

1. Click once after the period of the sentence you previously typed. Note the blinking text cursor indicating that the application is ready for you to enter text.

2. Type a space and then the sentence "Whenever the black fox jumped the squirrel gazed suspiciously."

3. Now go back to the "File" menu and select "Save" again. Seemingly nothing happens, but in fact something has happened. You've just saved the changes you made to your document. However, as you already told the application where to save the file and what the name is, it has no reason to ask you again by displaying a dialog box. It just overwrites the previous version of the document. A file save dialog box is only displayed the first time you save a document. From that point on, saving the file simply overwrites the current version.

4. Click the large "X" close box located in the upper right corner of the Notepad window. The application and your document disappear.

5. You've now created a document, saved it, added additional content, saved it again and closed the application. To open it again, go back to step 1 and open Notepad again.

6. With Notepad open, click on the "File" menu, then select "Open". A file open dialog box is displayed.

7. Now this dialog box is asking you "Where is the file that

you want to open located?" and, "What is the name of the file?" Remember that you saved the file in the "My Documents" folder. The "Save in" field of the save dialog box has been replaced with "Look in" for the open dialog box. Make sure "My Documents" is listed in this box. If not, click on the "My Documents" icon on the left side. Find the file named "my first document" in the right pane and either double-click on it or click once and then click the "Open" button. Either way is the same – your file is displayed. You've just re-opened a saved file. This is what you have to do to continue working on a document or just to display it.

8. Double-click on the word "brown" in your document – it becomes highlighted. Press the "delete" key to erase the highlighted word. You've now changed the document.

9. Click the large "X" close box in the upper right corner of Notepad. Instead of the document and application disappearing instantly as before, a dialog box is displayed.

10. Because the document contained an unsaved change, the application displays this dialog box alerting you that the document has changes not yet saved and asking if you'd like to save them now. Clicking "Yes" will save the changes and exit the program. Clicking "No" will not save the changes but will exit the program – losing all your changes forever. Clicking "Cancel" withdraws the click on the close box and acts like it never happened.

11. Click "Yes" to save your changes. The application closes along with your document.

12. Let's reopen the document, but this time we'll use an alternate method. Click on the "Start" menu, then click on the "My Documents" menu item. An Explorer window is displayed.

13. Double-click on the "my first document" icon. The file opens up in Notepad just as if you had opened Notepad and then selected "Open" from the "File" menu. Add a new sentence to the end of the document. Any sentence you wish to type is fine.

14. Select "Save As" from the file menu. A file save dialog box appears. The "Save As" command allows you to save a copy of a document to another file name, while leaving the original file untouched.

15. The original file name should be highlighted. Double-click the word "first" to highlight it and type "second" in its place. Click the "OK" button. If you were to click the "OK" button without changing the file name, you will get yelled at by the application. A error tone will sound and a dialog box will display, alerting you to the fact that a file already exists with that name and asking if you would you like to replace it. Files in the same folder must have unique names. Note that the Title Bar has changed to reflect the new document name.

16. Click the large "X" close box in the upper right corner to close the application.

17. Again, select "My Documents" from the "Start" menu. You'll now see the two documents that you have saved.

Your two saved
documents

The menu selection "Save as" is only used
to save a file under a new name. This is
equivalent to making a copy of the open file. If
the file has not previously been saved, meaning it is
newly created, selecting "Save as" is equivalent to
selecting "Save". Why would you want to save a file
under a different name? Well, you might want to create a
template or boilerplate, which is a bit of generic text,
and then add specific text to different versions. You
might also want to make significant changes to a
document without destroying the original just to see
how you like the changes. In fact, "Save as" is not used
all that often, but it is there if you need it.

Explorer

As you've already learned, most tasks on the PC can be done
in more than one way. This can be advantageous as chances

are you can figure out at least one way of accomplishing a needed task. On the other hand, the often bewildering number of options can overwhelm newbies.

Tasks related to file management, such as copying, deleting, and moving files, can be done in a variety of different ways. Which way you choose to use really depends on your personal preference. They all get you to the same place, but the journey is a bit different depending on which route you choose.

Most everything you do on the PC is either accomplished through selections on the Start menu, Quick Launch icons, or icons located on the Desktop. Occasionally however, you'll need to access a file that is not directly accessible through one of the above areas. In that case, you'll manually have to poke around the innards of the Windows file structure. This is done using Windows Explorer, either with or without the Taskpane. This was described briefly in the last chapter, but we'll take a detailed look here.

TOP SECRET The folks at Microsoft seem to *really* like the word "Explorer". It is a rather descriptive word, however, the multiple uses of this term can be really confusing to users. In an attempt to clarify all this, here is the deal:

Windows Explorer – An application that shows the hierarchical overview of all files and storage devices on the PC. Used to be a separate application in previous versions of Windows, but today is best thought of as a "view". It can be initiated by clicking the "Folders" button of any Desktop window.

Explorer Windows – If you select a folder, such as "My

Documents" from the Start menu, a window will open displaying the contents of the folder along with the Task Pane of hyperlinks described last chapter. I refer to this window as a "Desktop window", though I've seen it referred to as an "Explorer Window" which is extra confusing! If you click on the "Folders" button, the Task Pane is replaced by the Explorer hierarchical view.

Internet Explorer – The Microsoft web browser included with every copy of Windows, often abbreviated as "IE". I highly recommend *not* using IE and immediately replacing it with the free FireFox browser. See Chapter 7 for more details.

So, I'll use the term "Desktop window" for a window displaying a Task Pane, and Explorer for windows showing the hierarchical view. Again, you can change one into the other simply by clicking the "Folder" button.

Here are several ways to open or display (same thing) Desktop windows:

- Double-click the "My Computer" icon located on the Desktop.

- Select the "My Computer" icon located on the "Start" menu.

- Select any folder, such as "My Documents", "My Music", or "My Pictures" from the Windows Components area of the Start menu.

- Double-click any folder or storage device icon located on the right side of an already opened Desktop Window.

Select this menu item to display the contents of My Documents in a Desktop window

For example, selecting "My Documents" from the Start menu opens a Desktop window displaying the contents of the folder.

Notice the selected file named "Discover". When a file or folder is selected, a list of possible actions (hyperlinks) appear on the left hand side of the window in the Taskpane described in Chapter 3. Clicking on the action causes it to happen. For example, clicking on "Move this file" brings up the "Move Items" dialog box:

To complete the move, select the folder where you want to move the file, and click the "Move" button. Moving a file is exactly what it sounds like – it takes a file from one location and places it in another location.

Selected file

This method works fine if you're only moving one file. Otherwise, it can be cumbersome to navigate through various folders without an overall view of your hard disk and folder structure.

A better way, in my opinion, is to use the Windows Explorer

view. Explorer view or "Folders" view, allows for an overall view, a map if you will, of all the file storage mediums attached to your PC. These storage devices are your hard disks (main hard disk is labeled "C:"), and any other type of disk, such as floppy, CD-ROM or DVD.

Again, there are several ways to display the Explorer view.

● Click the "Folder" button located on the toolbar of any Desktop window.

 **Click the Folders icon to toggle Explorer view on and off**

● Shift/double-click any folder or disk icon.

● Right-click any folder or disk icon and select the "Explore" menu item.

● Select Start → All Programs → Accessories → Windows Explorer

My usual method of starting Explorer, is right-clicking on the Start menu and selecting "Explore". The main Explorer screen looks like this:

Essentially, Explorer is divided into two panes just like before. However, instead of hyperlinks or tasks, the left pane shows the hierarchical tree overview of disks and folders (also called directories). The right pane shows the contents of what is selected in the left pane; either files or other folders, sometimes called "sub-directories". Notice in the above example the "My Documents" folder is highlighted (selected) in the left pane, and the right pane shows what is inside the "My Documents" folder.

Storage devices and folders containing other folders in the left pane have a small "+' or "-" to the left of their names. Clicking on these signs either expands or collapses the hierarchical display. Let's take a look:

119

In the above graphic, all the items in the left pane have been collapsed. The Desktop, which is what appears on your monitor when you turn on your computer, is actually just a special folder. In the above screen shot, the Desktop is selected and the right pane shows the items residing on it. (Technically "in" the Desktop folder, but "on" is easier to visualize.) This begins to show you the overall architecture of the Windows operating system.

As you can see, Explorer gives you access to everything on your computer. The trick is to figure out which container (folder) contains the file you're looking for. This where Explorer comes in quite handy. It's much easier to find something when you have access to the overall view.

You're already at least somewhat familiar with the "My Documents" folder. Here's what happens if we click on "My Documents" in the left pane:

120

When the "My Documents" folder is selected, the folders contained within "My Documents" are shown below it in the left pane, and its folders and contents are displayed in the right pane. Note that "My Documents" contains twenty-four folders and two files, "Discover" and "open office user_guide"*. Of course, your "My Documents" folder will contain different items.

Notice that one of the folders is named "book stuff". This is a folder where I keep all my manuscripts, including this one. I draw your attention to this so that you could see a practical use of folders.

Remember our saving practice from the last section? We created two files; "my first document" and "my second document". Let's view those files again using Explorer this

---

* OpenOffice is a completely free suite of applications similar to Microsoft Office. Works great, in fact, this entire book was written and designed in OpenOffice. Check Chapter 8 for more info.

time.

1. Open Explorer by right-clicking on the Start menu located at the lower left-hand corner of the Desktop. Select "Explore" from the context menu.

2. Explorer opens. Click "My Documents" in the left panel right under "Desktop".

3. The contents of the "My Documents" folder are now displayed in the right-pane. Your contents will obviously vary from mine, though if you completed the above tutorial on saving files you should see the two files you created.

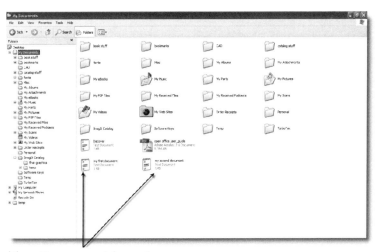

Two files created from the
previous section

Even if your "My Documents" folder did contain exactly the same files and folders as the graphic above, it may still appear differently. The way the files and folders are displayed is controlled by the menu option selected under the "View" Menu. More about "Views" later, but for now just make sure that "Tiles" has a check mark next to it.

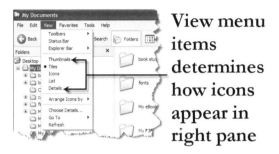

View menu items determines how icons appear in right pane

To get a feel for how all of this really works, let's go over a few common file manipulation tasks. In the last section you learned about saving files and navigating the hierarchical file structure of Windows from within applications. This section delves into the process of manipulating files outside of applications – using Desktop Windows and the Explorer or Folders view.

As you've probably figured out by now, folders are nothing more than containers – containers that exist for organization. If folders didn't exist, there would be only one container – the disk – and it would contain thousands of files.

So, with that in mind, let's use Explorer to organize the "My Documents" folder. First, we'll create a new folder for our recently created documents.

1. Open the "My Documents" folder if it is not already open.

2. Right-click in any blank area of the right pane.

3. Select "New" and then "Folder" from the context-menu. A new folder appears with the highlighted name of "New Folder". If you were to press the "Enter" key, the folder would retain this name, but type "test documents" in its place and then press "Return".

4. Now, place the two files we previously created into the new "test documents" folder. There are many ways we could do this. Let's try the click-and-drag method first. Click and drag the new folder so it is near the two files you created.

5. Click in a blank area of the right pane near the two files and while holding down the left mouse button, drag the selection rectangle to contain both files. Release the mouse button. Both files are now highlighted. This is difficult to describe but easy to do. Just try it. This is known as "contiguous selection".

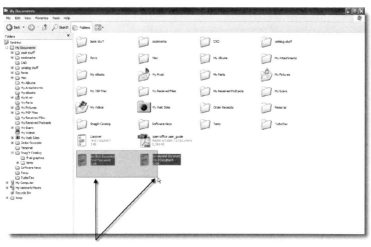

Click and drag diagonally until the selection box contains both files

124

6. Click and hold down the left mouse button on either file and drag the ghosted image over the folder you just created. The name of the folder will become highlighted when you are in the proper place. When that happens, release the mouse button. The files disappear – actually you've just moved them inside the new folder.

7. To verify this, double-click on the new folder to display the contents. Note that the Title Bar has changed to indicate the new folder name being displayed and that the new folder is highlighted in the left pane.

Folder name
Folder contents

New folder is now highlighted in left pane

Let's move the files back to their original location, but use a different way to do it.

1. Click on the first file in the right pane, it becomes selected. Hold down the control key (ctrl) and click the second file. Both files are now selected. This is an alternate way of

accomplishing extended selection and is useful when the files are not close to one another.

2. Click and drag the files over to the left pane until the pointer tip is directly over the "My Documents" folder. You'll know you're in the right spot when the folder name becomes highlighted. Release the mouse button and the files disappear from the right pane. The "test documents" folder is now empty and the files are back in their original folder.

3. Click on the "My Documents" folder in the left pane to display its contents and see the files you just moved there.

TOP SECRET You might never guess, but Windows is set up to hide certain information by default. Most folders contain hidden files and all files have hidden extensions – that is the last four characters of a file name. These extensions consist of a "." and three letters that indicate the type of file. These elements are hidden by default so as not to confuse people, and in general, this is a good theory. The file extension associates a file with a specific application. For example, a file with an extension of ".txt", which is a plain text file, is associated with Notepad. This is particularly useful as double-clicking on a data file will open the file using the associated application. Generally, the application is going to be the one that created it, but not always.

For example, double-click on either one of your newly created files. What happens? Yep, Notepad opens with the file you clicked on displayed. This is due to the fact the Notepad creates "txt" files and is associated with that file extension. These associations are already configured for you and rarely, if ever, need changing. If you're curious how they are changed though, go to: "My Computer", Tools→Folder Options... "File Types" tab. Changing these is not recommended unless you absolutely know what you're doing. Check my other book "I Just Want It To Work!" for details.

For our last file manipulation trick, let's rename a file.

1. Click once on the file "my first document" to select it. The file becomes highlighted.

2. Click once more on the file name itself. Just the file name becomes selected, indicating that the name can now be changed.

3. Type "my third document" and press the enter key. The file name is changed.

TOP SECRET It's really unavoidable – you're going to create a file (or download it), save it, and not be able to find it. It happens to everyone – some people quite frequently. The most common scenario for a new user is receiving an e-mail with attached files, saving them, and then having no idea where they are or how to view them again. Regardless of the specific scenario here's how to avoid and rectify the problem.

Whenever you save something by selecting File→Save (or Save As) think about the two things you will always have to provide when saving any file:

● **Location – Where the file will be saved.**

- File name – What the file name will be.

Say to yourself, "Where in my file cabinet (hard drive or other drive) do I want to save this file?" In answering this question, consider the type of file you're saving. Is it a picture? A logical place would be the "My pictures" folder located inside the "My documents" folder. If you're saving pictures of your grandkids, you might even further organize things by creating a folder named "grandkids" inside the "My Pictures" folder. After selecting and navigating to the location, say to yourself "What meaningful name can I give this file?" Even if you accidentally save a file in the wrong place (meaning you can't remember), you'll still be able to find it. If you don't know the name of the file and its name is meaningless, it will be extremely difficult (but not impossible) to find it.

For example, digital cameras are very useful and popular. The pictures are usually uploaded to a PC for viewing, sending to friends, etc. Unfortunately, these pictures are named by the camera when they are created and tend to have meaningless names like "dsc1344547-7575.jpg". Obviously this file name gives no clue of what it contains, however the ".jpg" extension does indicate a graphic format called jpeg, a type of picture. Most people don't rename these files before e-mailing them and not coincidentally, lots of people "lose" them once they receive them.... Of course this situation is easily avoided by renaming the files either when you save them, or by renaming them later while in a Desktop Window.

So make sure you give every file you save a meaningful name! File names in Windows XP can be up to 255 characters and can contain spaces. Some special characters cannot be used in file names, such as ":" and "\".

So, to avoid "losing" a file always intelligently consider where you are going to save the file and what you're going to name it.

All of that is well and good, but for whatever reason, you've lost a file. What to do? Lucky for you, Windows XP has a built-in search function. Refer to Chapter 13 "Step-By-Step" for instructions on finding files.

To create a new folder when saving a file, click the "New Folder" button, then type a name for the new folder and hit "Enter". Double-click the newly created folder so it appears in the "Save As" box and save file as normal

And one other thing, by default Windows XP already has an area set aside for files you create: My Documents. This is a folder and inside of My Documents exist other folders such as "My Music", "My Videos" and "My Pictures". You are free to create as many folders as you like. To further organize your files, create folders within "My Documents" for specific projects or categories. You can create them as illustrated above, or you can create them when you save your documents. The save dialog box offers a toolbar icon for creating a folder prior to saving a document.

I recommend using "My Documents" for all the files you create or save. It is a good way to organize a disk drive – segregating data files away from application and system files. In addition, many applications automatically default to the "My Documents" folder so you won't have to change anything.

Chapter 5

Application Basics

Oops! I almost left this chapter out. Once you understand the basics of saving and opening files, and how to operate the various Windows controls outlined in Chapter 3, what more could you need to know?

As it turns out, quite a bit. During one of my "computer tutoring" visits, my Mom vehemently pointed out that just because you know how to operate the controls doesn't mean you know what to do with them.

It is beyond the scope of this introductory text to explain the how-tos of every available application. Indeed, that would be virtually impossible and is one reason that bookstore shelves are packed with thick books on specific applications.

Back in the day – hey, I sound like my dad talking about walking to school in three feet of snow – computer programs actually came with useful printed documentation – in other words, instructions. These instruction manuals not only described how each menu command and tool functioned, but also included lengthy, step-by-step tutorials that were really helpful in teaching new users how to use the software.

Today however, the situation is much different. Software rarely comes with any printed documentation at all. That which does exist is usually a terse page or two on installing the program – sometimes titled something like "quickstart".

These "quickstart" manuals may be enough for seasoned veterans, but newbies are left out in the cold when it comes to learning. Note I said "may be enough". Again, the hundreds of thick books (really instruction manuals) for sale might lead you to believe otherwise....

So, while it's not possible to describe the specific functions of applications here, some generalizations mixed with a bit of common sense *and* some "let's see what happens if I try this", will go a long way.

Standardized Menus

Obviously, different types of applications and different brands of applications (for instance, Wordperfect and Microsoft Word word processors) use different menus and different menu commands.

However, there are some guidelines programmers follow when designing programs, and most programs do have a few standard functions.

The File Menu

Virtually all applications have a File menu and it is normally the first menu on the menu bar. As you might deduce, the File menu contains commands used to manipulate files.

The File menu is where the Save, Save as, Open, New and Close commands are found. Use these commands when starting a new project or saving one you're currently working on.

If you've just started the program and have no idea what to do next, the file menu is a logical place to begin. Look for a "New" command near the top of the file menu. This will create a new "whatever". For instance, selecting the "New" command in a word processor will create a new blank document. Likewise, selecting "New" in a solitaire game will create a new game to play.

The File menu also contains printing related menu commands. Use these to alter printer settings (if you have a printer attached) or to actually initiate printing.

The Exit command is also located on the File menu as the last menu command. Choose this command to shut down the program when you are finished working with it. Alternatively, you can also click the red "X" icon in the upper right corner of the window. If whatever you're working on is unsaved or you've made changes since it was last saved, selecting "Exit" or clicking the "X" icon will display a dialog box asking if you want to save your work. This prevents closing a document and losing your work.

The Edit Menu

Most programs also have an Edit menu. Edit commands are very specific to the type of project or document the application creates. No two edit menus are ever the same.

However, there are a few commands that are universal and those are cut, copy, and paste.

Cut, Copy, and Paste

Cut, copy, and paste are tools or functions that are available in virtually every application as well as the Windows XP operating system itself. These functions are essential elements to using a PC, yet many experienced users do not have a clear understanding of how these commands work. Ironically, the concept of cut, copy, and paste is one of the easiest to understand.

Simply put, cut, copy, and paste allow you to select objects (pieces of text, files, graphics, virtually anything) and move them somewhere else. This "somewhere else" could be another place in the same document, a different document open in the same application, or a completely different type of document in a different application. This saves you the effort of recreating already existing data and allows for editing after the data has been created.

For instance, suppose you have written an e-mail to a friend and you'd like to send part of that e-mail to your Mother. You could retype the needed portion into a new e-mail addressed to your mother. However, this would be a needless waste of time and energy – computers are supposed to be huge time-savers, right? Instead, you simply select the portion of text you wish to reuse in the e-mail to your mother, choose the "copy" menu command from the edit menu, and paste it into the new e-mail. This takes maybe five seconds once you're familiar with the procedure.

These commands work via an operating system feature called the "clipboard". You may occasionally hear this referred to as, especially by "old-timers", the "buffer".

The clipboard is an invisible (at least to you) storage or staging area. The size of this storage area depends on the physical RAM of your particular PC. It is handled automatically by the operating system. You never have to worry about starting or maintaining the clipboard. It is vigilantly standing by ready for use.

When you cut or copy an object, it is stored in the clipboard for future use. It will remain in the clipboard until one of two things happens:

- You restart or shutdown the PC

  or

- You cut or copy another object – this replaces the current object in the clipboard

Aside from these two things, whatever you place in the clipboard will remain there quietly waiting for you to use it at some point in the future.

A few things to keep in mind about cut, copy, and paste:

- Almost every application offers cut, copy, and paste.

- These commands are always located on the Edit menu.

- Many times these commands can also be found on the context menu displayed by right-clicking the selected item.

- Pasting generally occurs at the cursor's present location.

- Cut removes the selected object from the document and places it on the clipboard. If you inadvertently select "cut" when you really wanted to select "copy", simply select "paste" to put it back to where it was.

- Copy leaves the selected object where it is and places a copy of the object on the clipboard.

- Pasting between applications may give unexpected results. Because not every application handles text and graphics formatting the same, there may be some inconsistencies.

But it never hurts to try! (Pressing ctrl-z instantly undoes your last action – such as pasting).

- There are standard keyboard commands for cut, copy, and paste. They are ctrl-x, ctrl-c, and ctrl-v respectively. These are some of the few keyboard commands I have actually memorized and use constantly. Remember, the first two commands, cut and copy, work on selected objects only.

Cut, Copy, and Paste Exercises

These functions are so important to overall computer proficiency, I am including three step-by-step examples. Learning these will greatly increase your efficiency when using a PC.

Open Notepad again as illustrated in Chapter 4.

1. Type the following sentence: "The quick brown fox jumps over the lazy dog."

2. Select the entire sentence.

3. Select "Cut" from the edit menu. The sentence disappears and has been placed on the clipboard for future use.

4. Select "Paste" from the edit menu and the sentence reappears.

5. Now select "Paste" again. Another copy of the sentence occurs after the first one. This is because the copy is still on the clipboard. Select "Paste" several times to see how this works. Remember this copy will remain on the clipboard until the computer is restarted, shut down, or something else is copied to the clipboard.

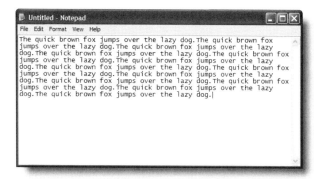

6. Now, clear all the sentences except for the initial one. (Select everything but the first sentence and press the "delete" key.)

7. Select just the word "brown". Either click and drag or double-click the word to select it.

8. Select "Copy" from the edit menu. Notice this time the selected text did not disappear. However, a copy has been made and placed in the clipboard. The word "brown" has now taken the place of the sentence that was previously there.

9. Place the cursor just before the word "dog" in the sentence.

10. Select the "Paste" command from the edit menu. Notice that the word "brown" is now inserted (pasted) in front of the word "dog". Cool, huh?

Though this example uses small pieces of text, you can see how useful this would be for moving large blocks of text around a document. Consider for a moment how these tools have changed the lives of writers. Years ago, if you were writing a book or any long document on a typewriter, you had to make sure that the order and sequence of your text was spot on or be prepared for many hours of rewriting the document. Today, that's all been changed. With a few mouse clicks you can reorder any document in just minutes!

Let's try another example. Imagine that you have a folder containing four pictures of your dog. Unfortunately, your digital camera named each picture file with a meaningless name (a number actually) and you've decided to rename the files. You could just rename each file as illustrated in Chapter 4 by typing each new name out manually. However, cut and paste would be much faster. You probably don't have a folder with four pictures just waiting to be renamed. You can try the following exercise on any files in the "My Documents" folder. Just remember to return them to their original names. You can easily do this by typing "ctrl-z" after you rename each file. This will "undo" the rename.*

1. Select the word "dog" from the document we just created and then select "Copy" from the Edit menu.

2. Click on the first file name to rename it – it becomes highlighted.

3. Now, right-click on the selected file name and select "Paste" from the context menu. Assuming you haven't shut down, restarted, or copied anything else to the clip board, the word "dog" will be pasted into the file name.

4. Following the word "dog" will be a blinking cursor. Type

---

* Crtl-z is the universal keyboard command for "undo" - it reverses the last action performed. Of course you know this from the previous chapter, right?

something meaningful like "outside" so the file name becomes "dog outside". Press return when done renaming the file.

5. Go to the next file and do the same thing typing something different after you paste the word "dog". See graphic below.

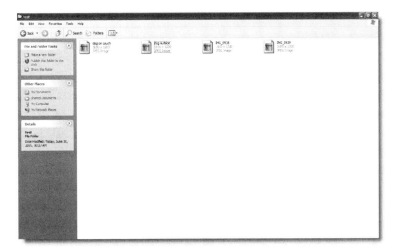

This final example not only reinforces the concept of cut, copy, and paste, but also illustrates an alternate way of moving a file. As we saw in Chapter 4, several ways of moving files exist. For example, you can use Explorer to drag and drop the file or you can also select the file, and click "Move this file" in the left pane. Here's how to do it with cut and paste:

Open the "My Documents" folder and navigate to the "test documents" folder we created earlier.

1. Right-click on a file.

2. Select "Cut" from the menu. The file becomes ghosted.

3. Use the "Back" arrow button to navigate back to the "My Documents" folder.

4. Right-click in any open area of the "My Documents" folder and select " Paste" from the menu.

5. The file you cut appears. You've just used cut and paste to move a file from one folder to another.

Note that had you selected "copy" in the above example instead of cut, you would now have identical copies of the file located in both folders. Go ahead and try it.

The Window Menu

The Window menu, if it is available, is used to control the display of open windows. Actually, it is used to organize the windows.

Applications can usually have more than one document open at a time. This can be very useful as it allows you to cut and paste between documents.

The actual menu commands available under the Window menu will vary by application. Usually there is a "Tile" and "Cascade" command.

The "Tile" command simply reduces the size of all open windows and tiles them next to each other so all are displayed on the screen at the same time.

Cascade reduces the size of each open window and places them in a stair-step arrangement so that the Title Bars are easily discerned. This makes it easy to click between windows.

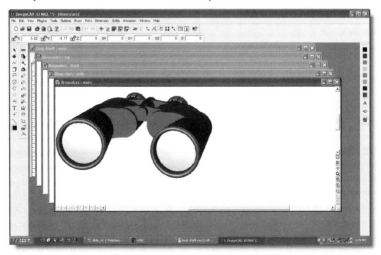

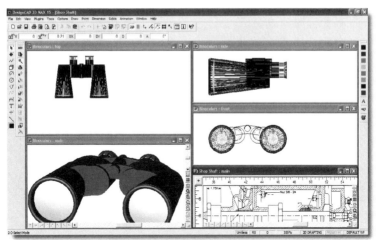

The Help Menu

The Help menu contains commands relating to, um, getting help. Again, commands on this menu are application specific and will vary.

Usually there is a command titled "Help" or "Contents". Selecting these commands displays a standard Windows help wizard.*

Note the usual Windows controls and the double-pane display. In these respects, the help wizard is remarkably similar to Windows Explorer which we examined in Chapter 4.

You can browse help topics by using the expand and contract controls (+ and − signs) located in the left panel. Clicking a topic displays the help information in the right panel.

You can also search for specific words by clicking the "Search" tab in the left panel and entering one or more search terms.

---

* "Standard" in this context is relative. There are some specific differences, but the general idea is the same.

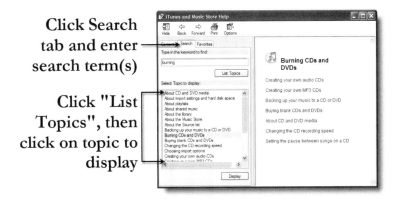

Click Search tab and enter search term(s)

Click "List Topics", then click on topic to display

A few other things to know about the Help menu:

● The universal keyboard command for displaying the help wizard, if the application offers one, is pressing the F1 key.

● Some applications will attempt to connect to the Internet and display a website with help. Many applications offer a standard help wizard with an additional menu command to obtain additional help from the developer's website.

● The last menu command on the Help menu is almost always "About" and will display version information for the application, such as OpenOffice Version 2.0014.

Standardized Toolbars and Controls

Tools and toolbars also vary depending on the application. Many tools are redundant in that they can also be selected by menu commands. Cut, copy, and paste can usually be selected by clicking on a toolbar's icons or menu selections. Choose whichever works for you.

Any applications that work with text will usually have controls for controlling the font (typeface), font size, font color, and font effects such as bold, italic, and underline.[*]

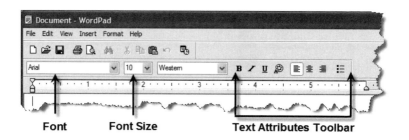

Font   **Font Size**   **Text Attributes Toolbar**

The above graphic is a screen shot of WordPad, a basic word processor included with every copy of Windows. You can find it by going to **Start menu→accessories→WordPad**.

Notice the forth line from the top starting at the left side. In order, you'll see drop-down boxes for font, font size, and language type. (basically useless if you speak and write in English) Followed by a series of icons on the toolbar.

To select a font or font size, use the drop-down box to make a selection. Note that if no text is selected, the change you make will take effect from that point forward and will be in effect until you change it to something else. If text is selected, the change will only affect the text you have selected.

The icons on the toolbar are, from left to right, bold, italic, underline, color, align left, align center, align right and bullets.

---

* Technically "font" means a combination of typeface along with qualities such as size, pitch, spacing and other attributes. While "typeface" is a collection of coordinated characters. In reality, these two terms have become synonymous – use whichever one you like....

Bold, *italic* and underline change the appearance of text, also known as "text attributes". Each can be used by itself or in combination with one or more attributes.

All three of these attributes work as toggles. That is, they remain active until you click the icon again to turn it off. Each of these attributes should be used sparingly. Usually you'll type a bunch of text, then go back and select a few words to make bold, italic, or underlined.

The three alignment icons change how paragraphs are displayed. Take a look at the next three paragraphs to see these three alignment options in action.

This paragraph is left-aligned, also referred to as "left-justified". Notice how the text is flush only on the left side, while the right side is ragged.

This paragraph is center-aligned, also referred to as "center-justified". Full lines of text are flush on both the left and right side, but shorter lines are located in the center of the page.

This paragraph is right-aligned, also referred to as "right-justified". In this case, the right side is now flush and the left side is ragged.

Many programs that format text also offer a fourth alignment choice known as "fully justified", or simply "justified". The text of this book is justified – text is flush with both left and right margins.

For most documents, you'll use either left-aligned or fully justified. Center justified is useful for making headlines.

The bullets icon places a bullet in front of each new

paragraph as shown below.

- This is a bullet list. Hit "enter" and another bullet appears.

- Not all programs offer bullet lists.

- Some programs allow the user to select the bullet symbol.

- Some programs allow the user to make numbered lists as well.

Putting It All Together

After watching my Mom struggle to use new applications, it became very clear that even though someone knows how to operate Windows controls, understands file basics, and even understands what a program is supposed to do or create, they probably have no idea of how to get started.

For the purposes of this discussion, let's divide application software into two rough groups; "Creating" software and "Viewing/Listening" software.* "Creating" software applications are used, not surprisingly, to create something. Word processors, greeting card programs (my Mom's favorite), graphics programs, desktop publishing programs, video editing programs, web page editing programs, spreadsheets and databases would all be examples of

---

* Grouping software into two groups, creating and viewing, is less than ideal. There are thousands of applications, many of which really don't fit perfectly in either category. For example, e-mail clients are both creating, you create e-mails, and viewing, you can view e-mails that are sent to you. Not a big deal as I am just trying to get you to visualize how a program is used. Oh, and hopefully this explanation will prevent you from e-mailing me about programs that don't fit in either category.....;-) Don't forget to check Chapter 8 for more specific information on different applications.

applications used to create something. "Viewing" software applications are used to view or listen to files. Music players, such as iTunes, MusicMatch Jukebox, and Winamp are used to listen to music files. Quicktime, RealPlayer, and Windows Media Player all play video files. Other "viewing" category software include, e-mail clients, web browsers, and graphic file viewers such as those included with digital cameras.

To use software in the "creating" category, you must adopt a certain mindset. This mindset, or general theory, goes like this:

- **You create a new "whatever"**. This could be a text document, graphic, web page or whatever it is that the program creates. Let's call this generic "whatever" a document as I have in the past. Most programs automatically open with a new, blank document ready to go. With a few applications, you might have to select "New" from the file menu.

- **You add or create content**. Here, you are either using the program's tools to create content, text, graphics, etc, from scratch, or you use "import" and/or cut and paste to add already existing content into your document.

- **You edit the content using the tools of the application**. This is usually accomplished by selecting an object – portions of text, a graphic, a spreadsheet cell – and then choosing a menu command or clicking a tool icon. This is an important point and one that many people overlook. If something doesn't work the way you think it should, make sure that the appropriate object is selected. Tool icons and menu commands are commonly "ghosted out" (dimmed) and unavailable for use unless the correct object is selected.

- **You save the project**. Of course you'll want to save your project when you are completely finished, but you may also want to save it several times before you finish so as not to lose your valuable work. In fact, it's perfectly acceptable and quite common to initially save a newly created project with an appropriate name right from the start. Many applications also offer the ability to automatically save your document on a schedule, say every 15 minutes. This way if you were to suffer a power outage or other catastrophe, you'll never lose more than 15 minutes of work.

With the above in mind, when you are faced with an unfamiliar program, ask yourself questions relating to the above points. What am I creating here? How do I open a new project? How do I create or add the content I want? Now that I have added or created some content, how do I change things to my liking?

By asking yourself these questions and breaking each task down into simple steps, you'll be able to figure out most applications.

Software in the "Viewing/Listening" category is designed to display or play certain kinds of files. There are dozens of file formats for images, audio, and video. Many players support multiple types. The following table shows the most common file types you are likely to run across. It is not necessary to understand the differences or meanings of each file type, only to know that you need specific players for specific file formats.[*]

---

[*] By default, Windows XP is configured to hide file extensions – file types. You can still find out the file type of any file without turning on "show file extensions" (See Chapter 4). This can be done by right-clicking the file, and selecting "Properties". A dialog box will display.

Image File Types	Audio File Types	Video File Types
jpeg – Joint Photographic Experts Group	mp3 – Motion Picture Experts Groups audio layer 3	qt/mov - Quicktime
gif – Graphic Interchange Format*	wav – Windows Audio Volume	avi – Audio/Video Interleaved
tiff – Tagged Image File Format	aiff – Audio Interchange File Format	mpeg – Various Movie Pictures Expert Group file formats

The second line from the top will show "File Type".

* Proof of people with too much time on their hands follows: Once you successfully get online, you'll find information on topics that will be difficult to comprehend. Hence, the word "gif". The gif file format was introduced by CompuServe in 1987 and has become something of a web standard. Ever since it was introduced, people have been arguing over the correct pronunciation. Seriously. Internet forums, sometimes referred to as "bulletin boards" were rife with "flame wars" (arguing) about this topic. Chat rooms were alive with this discussion. Personally, I worked with an individual who was obsessed with people using the correct (in his mind at least) pronunciation. What really made it fun was that there was another employee who insisted on using the other pronunciation. All of which resulted in employee number one spending an entire afternoon searching the web until he finally found a quote from the original developer of the format explaining how to pronounce it. Sigh. Anyway, it is either pronounced "jif" as in Jif peanut butter, or with a hard "g" as in gift. My take? Pronounce it how ever you'd like.... Oh, and if *yo u* have too much free time, you can still read all about that debate at: http://www.olsenhome.com/gif/

149

Image File Types	Audio File Types	Video File Types
bmp - Bitmap	cdda – Compact Disk Digital Audio	rm – Real Media
	wma – Windows Media Audio	wmv - Windows Media Video
	ra – Real Audio	
	qt - Quicktime	
	aac – Advanced Audio Coding	

Popular applications in the Viewing/Listening category include:

● iTunes – A free music application distributed by Apple that plays music files of various formats such as MP3 and AAC. With iTunes, you can also connect to the Apple iTunes store and purchase music to download for $.99 per song.

● Quicktime – Another Apple product. Quicktime plays video files in several formats. The basic version is free.

● Winamp – An MP3 music player. Free for basic version, $14.95 for pro version which can "rip" music into MP3 format.[*]

* "Ripping", in this context means encoding a music CD into MP3 format. This is useful for converting CDs you already own into portable music files that can be played on your PC or MP3 player.

- Real Player – Plays various music and audio files including "Real movie format". The basic version is free. Tends to install many extra pieces and parts, some of which can be annoying.

Also note that Windows XP includes two "player" type applications; Windows Media Player and Windows Picture and Fax viewer.

Windows Media Player, or WMP, plays a variety of popular audio and video formats. In addition, WMP is expandable by installing "codecs" - small programs that allow WMP to play certain file formats.

Windows Picture and Fax viewer is a rudimentary program that doesn't do much more than display pictures. It supports a few of the most popular formats and is adequate for occasional use. And the price is certainly right – it's free!

As you become more proficient using the PC, you will be better able to evaluate your software needs and choose whatever is right for you.

When it comes to obtaining "player" type applications, I recommend searching online software sites such as www.download.com. Many free and shareware applications are available and most work quite well, but be careful! Make sure you read Chapter 10 first. Oh, and if you purchase a digital camera, chances are very good it will include a nice, full-featured image viewer/organizer application. Many of the new, all-in-one printer, scanner, copier machines also include excellent image software.

Just like software in the "creating" category, to use software in the "Viewing/Listening" category you need to adopt a certain mindset, a mental-map of how these applications work. This is much less complex than with "creating" software.

● **You start the application**

● **You open or load the file you want to play or display**. Note that these first two steps can be combined by double-clicking on a data file. Remember that this opens the file and the application associated with this particular file type.

● **You play the file or portion(s) of the file that you desire**

That is pretty much it, though some players have built-in organization features. This allows you to keep a library of files, view and create playlists or slide shows, and organize similar files by category.

For example, let's take a look at iTunes, a popular audio file player.

It may look confusing at first, but soon you'll see that the screen resembles Windows Explorer in a number of ways. The left pane contains the main library and playlists. The right lower pane lists all the music files contained in whatever is selected in the left pane. The three upper right panes display the music contained within the library by genre, artist, and album.

To play, select an object(s), be it an individual songs or play list(s) and use the movie controller located in the upper left corner.

Player Controls

Library and Play Lists

Song Files

To add music files and create playlists, use the "File" menu.

You can also print playlists and import songs from CDs you already own by using this menu.

TOP SECRET Ok, so it's not exactly a secret. In fact, I've mentioned it before, but it bears mentioning again while we're on the subject of players. Remember that if you double-click on a file it will open with the application associated with it. So, if you have iTunes installed and you double-click on an

MP3 file, iTunes will open and begin playing the file. This is particularly useful when downloading video and audio files from the Internet. Much of the time, especially with video files, you'll watch them once and then discard them so they don't take up disk space. In this case it makes sense to download these files to the Desktop, double-click to play, then drag them to the Recycle Bin when finished. Oh, and one other thing, if your PC doesn't have a player for a particular file type, a dialog box will be displayed asking you to select an application to play the file. In most cases you'll have to obtain a player for that specific file format.

Chapter 6

Does This Thing Come With Internet?

Perhaps the foremost reason most people are interested in purchasing and learning to use a PC is to get online – AKA the Information Super-highway, Cyberspace, The Web.

Regardless of how the media is referring to it nowadays, getting connected to the Internet is definitely something you'll want to do. You will be able to send and receive e-mail, play online games with people from around the world, instantly check weather and stock quotes and look up in-depth information on any topic.

Unfortunately for the uninitiated, getting online can be a bit, let's just say ,"tricky".

Just What is This Internet Thing Anyway?

Just what is "online" you ask? What is this thing that you constantly hear about called the Internet?

The Internet is nothing more than a network of networks. And networks are nothing more than computers connected to other computers for the purpose of exchanging information. No one owns the Internet itself, though people and organizations own individual pieces, such as the computers (called servers) and the infrastructure such as communications lines. The whole thing is overseen by a non-profit society whose job is to standardize protocols and make sure everything flows smoothly.

Getting Connected

To get yourself online, you really only need two things: a PC, and an "ISP" – an Internet Service Provider. Sounds scary, huh?

An ISP is simply the company, could be your phone or cable company, could be America Online (which you've probably at least heard of), or a small local company which, for a fee, provides you with a connection to the Internet. These companies are the middle man between your computer and the Internet.

As soon as you get involved with the Internet, you're going to hear the terms "upload" and "download". These terms refer to the transferring of files from one computer to another. If you are receiving a file from another computer, you're downloading. If you're sending a file to another computer, you're uploading.

There are a few different types of ISPs:

- **Hi-speed Providers** – Also known as "broadband" providers. For most households in the U.S., there are two options for broadband Internet access: DSL (Digital Subscriber Line) and cable (provided along with cable TV). A third option, wireless, is also occasionally available. Broadband Internet access is definitely what you want. Broadband access is much faster than dial-up. This means you spend less time waiting for web pages to load, and e-mails and programs to download. With broadband, you can listen to music and radio programs and even watch videos. In addition, broadband is an "always on" connection. With dial-up access, you must instruct your computer to dial an access number as needed. This takes around a minute and makes your phone line busy to incoming calls. With broadband, there is no dialing – you're always connected to the Internet and your phone line is always free. The downside to broadband is that it is more expensive. Prices are coming down however. With the increased competition between phone and cable companies, the price differential can be almost negligible.

- **AOL** – America Online is one of the countries largest ISPs. At one point, AOL offered both dial-up and broadband service. Apparently, they are now only offering dial-up access. I am not a fan of AOL. It is one of the most expensive providers out there, and in my opinion they market towards novices who don't really know any better. AOL uses a proprietary software interface for connecting, though once connected you can use more generic software, such as the FireFox or Internet Explorer browsers. There are two things that AOL does have going for it: thousands of local dial-in numbers and ease of use. Note that in addition to dial-up service, AOL offers "AOL for Broadband". Notice the "for" in that phrase. In this case, you have to have a broadband provider as outlined above. AOL for broadband is just their software interface. It is a waste of money and not necessary. Skip it.

- **Dial-up ISPs** – If you can't get broadband (most of the U.S. can) you're stuck with either AOL or another dial-up provider. The others differ from AOL in that they do not provide a proprietary software interface. You create a connection through Windows with information the ISP will provide, and then use whatever software you want to connect. This is the way to go *if* you cannot get broadband, though this route is slightly less user-friendly than AOL.

If you have the choice, go with a high-speed broadband provider. You may have the choice between several broadband providers. Ask friends, family, and co-workers for recommendations in your area.

In fact, you may be lucky enough to have access to both DSL and cable broadband. Generally, DSL tends to have less service interruptions (it's piggybacked on your phone connection) and more stable speed. Most DSL providers offer a tiered service based on the speed you want, with faster service being more expensive. The slowest DSL offered is usually 384 downstream/128 upstream and is adequate for most home users, though faster is always better. Ask if those speeds are guaranteed.

TOP SECRET Once you're actually online you can test the speed of your connection by pointing your browser to www.auditmypc.com/internet-speed-test.asp and clicking on "Start".

Broadband via cable is a "shared" technology, meaning whenever your neighbors go online you share the bandwidth with them. At peak usage periods, defined as "whenever you want to go online", throughput can greatly slow. Sometimes the speed can drop to hardly above dial-up speed. Read the fine print. Cable companies like to bandy about impressive sounding speed numbers such as "twice as fast as DSL...". While technically this is possible, it rarely happens in reality. Cable companies rarely, if ever, guarantee speed ratings. Also consider how often your cable TV "goes out". When cable TV is down, generally so is cable Internet access.

If you are brand new to using a PC, getting online can be a

confusing and daunting prospect. Ideally, a tech-savvy friend or family member can be recruited to get you set up and online.

If you simply don't have anyone to help you, your choices are paying someone to help you, or doing it yourself. If you have chosen a broadband ISP, you may be able to get a technician to install the service and get you started. Some broadband providers offer several options for installation, including self-install (usually free) and onsite technician install (usually costs extra). If you feel that you need help, paying a small amount for a technician to get you started is well worth it. There is one forewarning to this: Some providers (notably SBC here in the mid-west region) will charge considerably more to customers selecting a technician install from the start. For example, if you choose self-install which is free, and consequentially can't get it to work, SBC will send out a technician to complete the install for $150. This is in contrast to selecting a technician install from the start which costs $200. In a case like this, I recommend attempting the self-install yourself. Even if you can't figure it out (it's not that hard) you save $50!

Cable broadband providers often send a technician out to perform the install automatically with any account. This could be a selling point to some. Be sure and ask before you sign up.

Dial-up providers rarely offer onsite technical support and instead offer phone support. Setting up a dial-up connection is not difficult, as Windows XP provides a wizard to assist with this task (See Chapter 11 for details). It really requires nothing more than clicking buttons and entering information provided to you by the ISP.

If you do decide either by choice or necessity to get online by yourself, here are a few things to keep in mind:

- **Be cautious of "bait and switch" deals.** Many ISPs advertise great sounding deals such as "First 6 months for $19.95". Find out what the real monthly cost is and also how long the sign-up agreement lasts. Many ISPs are now requiring a one year contract. This isn't necessarily a bad thing if the price and service are right for you.

- **Most ISPs do provide step-by-step instructions when you sign up.** Follow these to the letter! Skipping a seemingly small detail could cause the entire install to fail. This is one time you really do need to read the instructions.

- **If you have trouble, call the provided tech-support number.** If they are unable to resolve your problem, call the sales department and request help. Often the sales department will put pressure on the tech support department to avoid losing a sale.

- **With a dial-up account, a phone line is needed to plug into the computer's modem connector.**

- **DSL accounts will also need access to a phone line.** The phone line is then plugged into the DSL modem (supplied with your account) and a separate network cable is then plugged into the computer's Ethernet port. Most new computers have Ethernet built-in, while some older computers will need a plug-in card called a Network Interface Card or NIC.

- **Your ISP will provide you with a username, password,**

and e-mail account information.[*] Be sure to write this information down somewhere you will remember. Your e-mail address will be in the form of whateveryouselect@Internetprovider.com. For example, joesmith@isp.com. Generally, you won't be able to change your username or e-mail address once you've selected them. Make a list of usernames and e-mail addresses you would like before signing up.

● **If you have someone knowledgeable help get you initially connected to the Internet, ask them to download and install the FireFox browser and ZoneAlarm firewall.** See Chapter 10 for more information.

TOP SECRET Wireless broadband Internet access is available is some areas. If it's your only choice, definitely consider it. The wireless ISP will provide you the information and equipment you need.

Related to, but not the same as broadband wireless is "WIFI". This is a completely different type of wireless access, and is also referred to as "802.xx" protocol. Whereas broadband wireless provides a connection between your home and the ISP, WIFI is a connection between a computer and an access point and is used for relatively short distances. The most common usage of WIFI is connecting a wireless access point (around $50) to your broadband Internet connection. This allows you

---

[*] You'll probably want to set up a file somewhere safe (perhaps with your financial records) to store pertinent computer information, specifically usernames and passwords. Once you get online, you'll be creating and using lots of these for various websites. Check Chapter 10 for more information.

to use a WIFI-enabled PC, most likely a laptop, to connect to the Internet from anywhere within a 300-500 foot range. For example, you could check the Internet news and weather sites from your backyard deck. In essence, WIFI works somewhat like a typical cordless phone. It replaces the wire connection with a two-way radio.

To set up a WIFI home network, you'll need the following:

● A broadband Internet connection

● A wireless access point

● A PC with a built-in WIFI adapter or a WIFI network card

Here's a tip that might very well save you some money: Share a broadband Internet connection via WIFI with your neighbors and split the cost. If you're physically close to your neighbors, such as in a condo or townhouse, you might consider having one person obtain a broadband connection and then share that connection via WIFI with other neighbors. This is easy to do. The only requirement is that everyone sharing the connection has to have WIFI-enabled computers.

In addition to home WIFI networks, many commercial establishments are now offering WIFI "hotspots". These are wireless access points that you can connect to, thus allowing you to connect to the Internet. Starbucks coffee shops, Border's, and Barnes and Noble bookstores all offer WIFI hotspots for a small fee. Panera, a popular cafe with locations in many states, offers WIFI Internet

access free of charge. Check www.panera.com for a location near you.

Once you have your computer successfully connected to the Internet, what do you do? Well, the possibilities are virtually endless. First things first though. You'll want to learn how to view web pages, search for information, and send and receive e-mail. On to the next chapter!

Chapter 7

Browsing and E-mail

The World Wide Web

As discussed in Chapter 5, the Internet is a vast network of computers. These computers communicate using different protocols – standards used for communication. One of these protocols is the World Wide Web or www.

Special computers called web servers, hold web pages, several of which combine to make websites. Applications called "browsers" are used to display these pages.

There is obviously a bit more to it than this, but you don't need to know the intricacies of the internal workings. You just want to view web pages.

Viewing web pages is referred to by quite a few different names and phrases. The most popular are "surfing" and "browsing" – as in "surfing or browsing the web".

Browsing is just looking at web pages and clicking on hyperlinks. Once you are connected to the Internet via an ISP, all you need in order to browse is a browser. And a browser is just an application used to view web pages.

Windows computers come with a browser, Internet Explorer, installed. IE, as it is commonly referred to, certainly works, but I recommend switching to FireFox if you can. FireFox is free, simple to use, and very reliable. It also lacks many of the inherent security vulnerabilities of IE. Check Chapter 9 for a detailed tutorial of how to get and install FireFox.

Surfing

Regardless of the browser you have, surfing works pretty much the same way – start (open) a browser, enter a web address (URL) into the address bar, press the enter key and the page is displayed.*

Let's take a detailed look at these steps. The screen shots and specific instructions that follow are for the FireFox browser, but if you're using IE or even AOL it will still make sense. Feel free to follow along on your PC.

1. **Connect to the Internet if you are not already connected**. If you have a broadband connection you should always be connected. Dial-up users must dial and connect.

2. **Start/open the browser application**. Try and think of all the ways you could accomplish this. I usually start my browser by clicking the icon located on the Quick Launch bar or selecting it from the Start menu. You could also double-click the icon if it is on your Desktop. The icon for Internet Explorer is a large blue "e", shown below next to the FireFox icon.

3. **Click once in the address field**. A blinking text cursor

---

* "URL", pronounced "earl", stands for Uniform Resource Locator. In English: web address such as www.amazon.com.

appears or the address already there becomes highlighted. Type "www.smartguypress.com" and press the enter key. The SmartGuy Press web page is displayed. Congratulations! You're surfing the web!

Address Field

4. **Click on any of the hyperlinks on the SmartGuy web page and see what happens.**[*] Move the cursor slowly around the page until it becomes a hand with extended forefinger to find the hyperlinks. Hyperlinks should be obvious, but occasionally can be tricky to locate.

5. **Once you have played around with the links on the SmartGuy Press page, try entering other addresses into the address bar**. Try inserting brand names or generic words between www. and .com. Then try clicking on the hyperlinks on those pages.

---

* Hyperlinks, as you probably remember from Chapter 3, are words or images that you can click on to display a new page or portion of a page. Hyperlinks, or links as they are frequently called, are the primary method of navigation on the World Wide Web.

Searching The Web

When you get bored with the above (may take a long while, could be years....), try searching for websites on specific topics. Here's how:

1. **Enter the address of a search engine in the address bar of your browser**. Many search engines exist. Check Chapter 15 for a list. For now, use www.google.com. Press the enter key. The main Google search page is displayed.

2. **Enter the word "cats" in the search field and press the enter key or click the search button**. A new page is displayed with hyperlinks to other pages with information on cats.

3. **Browse the cat links or enter other search words**. Search! Click links! Explore! You won't break anything surfing web pages.

If you install and use the FireFox browser (and I highly recommend that you do), you can skip going to the search engine web page and enter the search term directly into the search field located in the upper right corner.

 Search Field

Note the small black triangle next to the "G". The "G" represents the Google search engine. Clicking on the triangle displays a drop-down list of available search engines. FireFox comes with several installed by default, such as Google, Amazon, Ebay, dictionary.com Several others can be installed by selecting "Add Engines..." from the drop-down list. I personally use Google for most of my searching activities, along with Ebay and Amazon for merchandise searches.

Click drop-down arrow to display list of search engines

E-mail

E-mail has revolutionized the way people communicate and is often reason enough to purchase a PC. E-mail is nothing more than an electronic note that is transmitted to another computer.

It is the speed and convenience of this electronic note that makes if far more useful than "snail mail".* Aside from the cost of the computer and the service fees for your ISP, e-mail is free. E-mail is almost instantaneous – you press the "send" button and the recipient should receive it almost instantly. I say "almost" and "should" in that sentence as there is no guarantee of instant delivery. General Internet as well as server specific slow-downs(your e-mail server or the recipient's) can cause e-mail to be delayed. E-mail has one other advantage over snail mail; you can attach files to it. This means you can send and receive pictures, music, and video – anything really.

To send and receive e-mail, you need a computer, a connection to the Internet, an e-mail account and the appropriate software.

---

* "Snail mail" is the term for regular USPS mail. Note that this is not a complimentary term....

E-mail accounts can be grouped into two categories; POP accounts and Web accounts. Technically, there is another type of mail account: IMAP – Internet Message Access Protocol. I haven't heard of many ISPs providing IMAP accounts, so we'll deal primarily with POP and Web accounts. Although you'll want to note that configuring an e-mail client to access an IMAP account is very similar to setting up a POP account.

POP is an acronym for "Post Office Protocol". A POP account holds your incoming mail on a special type of computer called a "mail server". Using a specific type of application known as a "mail client", you connect to the mail server and download your e-mail onto your computer. POP accounts generally offer more features than web accounts, though POP accounts are rarely free. Luckily, a POP account or accounts are usually included with your ISP account.[*]

Web accounts are typically free though most offer upgraded features, such as more storage space or spam-blocking, for a fee. Web accounts store your mail on the mail server – you don't download your mail onto your PC. In addition, no mail client software is used. Accessing webmail is done with a web browser, which does give you the advantage of being able to access it from virtually anywhere.

AOL mail doesn't really fit in either category. You only have AOL mail if you have selected AOL as your ISP. AOL mail is held on the mail server, and your account is accessed via the proprietary AOL software.

---

[*] Many ISP accounts come with several different mail accounts so that everyone in your family can have their own.

170

Using a POP Account

Using a POP account is very simple. Configuring a POP client can be somewhat less so.

To start you'll need a PC, a POP account and e-mail client software. Again, a POP account is probably included with your Internet service so check with them if you have any questions.

You'll need all the information provided by your ISP about your POP account. At a minimum you'll need the following:

● Username

● Password

● Incoming mail server

● Outgoing mail server (sometimes called "SMTP" server, which stands for "Simple Mail Transport Protocol")

The e-mail client software is most likely already installed on your PC. Microsoft Outlook or Outlook Express is installed by default on new Windows PCs. Another popular e-mail client is Thunderbird from the same people that distribute the FireFox browser. Thunderbird is available free from www.getfirefox.com. (Check Chapter 10 for downloading and install specifics.)

POP e-mail clients, while differing in specific features, work essentially the same way. After the client is installed, you enter the specific information provided by your POP account provider. After the client is configured, clicking on a "Get

Mail" button contacts the mail server, retrieves any new mail, and uploads any outgoing mail you've created.

Configuring The E-mail Client

You'll need a few pieces of information to set up your client. This information will be provided by the POP account provider, which is most likely your ISP also. Contact them if you have questions.

You'll need your e-mail username (most likely your address, such as joesmith@isp.com), password, incoming mail server and outgoing mail server.[*]

Let's walk through configuring an e-mail client. Regardless of what specific client you have, the procedure is generally the same. The screen shots below are from Thunderbird.

1. **Start your e-mail client**. You can most likely select the client icon from the Start menu, or by double-clicking its icon on the Desktop.

2. **Choose "Account settings" from the "Tools" menu.** The new account wizard appears. Select "E-mail Account" from the list and the "Next" button.

3. **Input your real first and last names and your e-mail address as provided by your POP account provider.** Your first and last name will appear on all e-mails you send.

[*] When you sign-up for a POP account, you will get to select the first part of your e-mail address. You can choose whatever you wish as long as an account with that exact name does not already exist. Choose something easy to remember and meaningful to you, such as first initial and last name.

4. **Continue to click "Next" and enter the requested information**. The fields are self-explanatory with the possible exception of "usernames". Depending on your POP provider this will either be the first part of your e-mail address, before the ".isp.com", or the entire e-mail address. Ask them if you are unsure.

Once the e-mail client is properly configured, sending and receiving e-mail is very straightforward.

Most POP clients are configured by default to automatically upload and download mail immediately when they are started. This setting is usually located under "Preferences" or "Options".

To send or receive e-mail manually, click the "Get Mail" button. This sends any mail you've written but not sent, as well as downloads any incoming e-mail from the server onto your PC.

Click "Get Mail" icon to send and receive mail

To create an e-mail, click the "Write" icon on the toolbar. A new message form appears.

Creating the e-mail is as simple as filling out the form.

The first line is where you enter the e-mail address of the recipient. You must have this address to send an e-mail. Note the additional lines for additional addresses. You can send one e-mail to several people at the same time. Also note the inverted triangle to the left of the address field. This displays

173

a drop-down list where you can select if a particular address should be a "cc", carbon copy or a "bc", blind copy. Be careful with these! Some people are very sensitive about being included on "cc" lists, particularly if you're forwarding something they have already written.

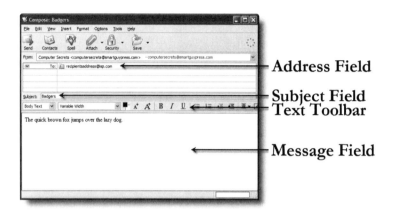

After the address, is the subject field. This is technically optional. If you don't enter anything, the e-mail will appear with <none> in the subject field. Take the time to enter a meaningful subject. This really helps the recipient to differentiate between spam and valuable e-mails. An interesting idea would be to describe what the e-mail is about....*sarcasm*

Next, is the e-mail body text itself. Write whatever you'd like just as if you are writing an actual letter. Don't forget to spell check! Most e-mail clients have a toolbar button for spell checking. The program will highlight all misspelled words and offer suggestions to correct them.

After you have finished writing the letter you have two options. You can click the "Save" button to display the save file dialog box or you can click "Send" to actually send the message. Saving only keeps the message on your computer. It does not send it.

Web-based E-mail

Web-based e-mail is extremely popular for a number of reasons. Foremost, it is free. You can have multiple accounts if you want and they will cost you nothing. The other big advantage of web-based e-mail is portability – you can send and receive e-mail through your web e-mail account from anywhere there's a computer, browser, and Internet connection. This can be very handy when traveling.

There are dozens of websites that offer free e-mail accounts. Try searching for "free e-mail". By far the most popular are Yahoo, Hotmail, and Excite. As this book goes to press, the search engine Google is testing a new concept in e-mail called Gmail. It's free and offers 2 GB of storage space. Check gmail.google.com for details.

To sign up for a free e-mail account, click on the appropriate links and fill out the requested information. I'd advise you to decline all the "special offers" or you will end up with a mailbox full of spam in a very short time.

TOP SECRET **The free e-mail providers will ask you for a ton of personal information. They also ask for a master e-mail address to hook the account to. You can make up whatever you like for these fields – nothing is verified. Actually, I recommend you enter false information anytime you're asked for personal information on the web. The bottom line is that your information belongs to you and no one has the right to demand any personal information from you. The**

more personal information you keep private, the less chance of identity theft. Keep your info out of as many databases as possible!

Once you sign up, you can send or retrieve your e-mail by using a web browser, entering the web address and logging

Email messages appear as hyperlinks. Click to read mail

on with your e-mail address and password. All e-mail tasks are handled through the browser and appear as hyperlinks.

E-mail Etiquette

Writing e-mail seems like nothing more than common-sense. Unfortunately, sense isn't all that common anymore, and when it comes to the Internet, sense is as rare as purple cats. Believe me, within weeks of getting an e-mail address you will have at least one friend or relative that sends you dozens of useless chainletters and urban legends. You may also receive countless e-mails written IN ALL CAPITALS SO IT SEEMS LIKE THEY'RE SHOUTING. Probably both.

Here's a few things to keep in mind when composing e-mail:

- **Put something useful in the "Subject" field**. With all

the spam and phishing (See Chapter 10) going on, it helps to use a meaningful subject so the recipient can easily ascertain that your e-mail should be opened.

- **I've said it before and I'll say it again: Think** *before* **you click**. In this case, think long and hard before you send a heated e-mail. Many jobs and friendships have been lost by sending out e-mails in the heat of the moment.

- **Don't send or forward chain e-mail**. It's all a bunch of garbage. Don't waste your friends' and family's valuable time.

- **Same thing goes for all the urban legends, animations, video clips, jokes and pictures that get forwarded to everyone.**[*] This type of stuff is easy to find and anyone interested in it has probably already seen it. Also, forwarding this kind of garbage to someone at work could get them into trouble.

- **Most e-mail clients have a spell check feature – Use it**. Communication via e-mail or Instant Messenger is all text. Misspellings and bad grammar reflect poorly on you.

- **Only use capital letters where appropriate**. "Where appropriate" is exactly as you learned in school. USING CAPITALS ELSEWHERE SEEMS LIKE YOU'RE SHOUTING. People generally don't like to be shouted at....

- **Be careful who you include in the carbon copy field**. The "cc" field, or even worse, the "bc" field is a simple way to send an e-mail to a bunch of people at once. Be

---

[*] You're bound to receive e-mails referring to urban legends. To find out whether they have any truth, surf over to www.snopes.com.

careful when forwarding e-mail you've received to other people.

- **Go easy on the "net speak" and smileys**. Since most people are not very proficient at touch-typing, much online communication is done by the use of abbreviations and "net speak".* Once online you're bound to see phases like "Omgilmao!", which means "Oh my god I am laughing my ass off!". And then there are the "smileys". Smileys are punctuation marks used to express emotions such as :-) which represents a smiley face. Tilt your head to the left to see it. Some instant messaging programs and AOL e-mail take the smileys and convert them into actual graphics. While both net speak and smileys are well established Internet conventions, use them sparingly, especially in e-mail. Both are more appropriate when chatting online.

- **Be careful about using unusual symbols, such as ™ and ©, or using formatting, such as colored , bold, and italic text in your e-mails**. Not all e-mail clients or webmail services decipher text the same way. Some allow the use of HTML tags – a markup language used to create web pages, some don't. Your best bet is to rely on plain text and save the fancy formatting and symbols for printed documents. Oh, and if you are using AOL, those cutesy graphic smiley faces will only be visible if they are read by someone else using AOL.

---

* Try out your new Internet skills by doing a web search for "net speak".

Chapter 8

Other Applications

Now you know how to e-mail, surf the web, and search for information. But there are many, many other tasks you can do with your computer. It would be virtually impossible to cover all the different types of computer applications in one book. Therefore I'll list the most common types and what they're used for. Also, now that you're online you can find additional information by searching the web.

Keep in mind that these applications are totally optional; you should only consider getting these programs if you have a definitive need. And be sure to read the section on shareware and freeware in this chapter. Chances are you can get totally free software off the Internet to do exactly what you need!

Text Formatting Applications

Aside from Internet applications, programs that manipulate text are the most popular.

Years ago there were two types of text manipulation programs; word processors and desktop publishing applications. The differentiation between these two types was the ability to incorporate and manipulate graphics along with text. At the time, word processors had little or no ability to do this.

Today the line is very blurred indeed, as word processors are very adept at combining graphics with text. Additionally dedicated desktop publishing programs have faded in popularity and are mostly used by magazine publishers.

Along with the ability to combine text with graphics, word processors now offer a prodigious set of features and wizards to create business cards, banners, greeting cards, T-shirts, newsletters, and address labels.

Besides Notepad, which is a very rudimentary word processor, chances are extremely high that your system already has another word processor installed, likely a "works version" (See below).

Microsoft Word and Corel WordPerfect are the two big word processors available for Windows PCs. Both are expensive and do far more than most people need. This means they take up disk space and are more difficult to use. If your PC comes with one of these installed at no extra cost, obviously you're out nothing and I recommend using whatever you have – at least to begin with. However, I wouldn't pay extra for either of these two programs.

Specialized Printing – Cards, T-Shirts, Banners

Many optional applications exist that are targeted at very specialized tasks – like creating greeting cards. There are many to choose from and once online you can check for reviews of applications you're interested in. Amazon.com in particular allow customers to post reviews of items they've purchased.

Before purchasing though, make sure that you really need a dedicated application to do what you want. Many specialized tasks, such as banner or tile printing, and printing custom T-shirt iron-ons can be created by a "works" or "suite" program. (Both explained later) The graphic below shows just a few of the specialized tasks offered by Microsoft Works.

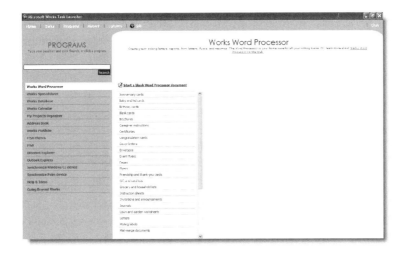

Almost any text/graphics program can be used to make T-shirt iron-ons. The key is not the application, but the fact that you need special iron-on paper to print on. You can purchase this transfer paper almost anywhere computer supplies are sold for around $1 a sheet. The only capability that the dedicated T-shirt applications, like T-Shirt Factory, offer over generic programs is the ability to print the design in mirror-image so it appears properly when ironed on. Be sure and check your current applications for this ability first. Also, some of the recently released printers offer this feature regardless of the program used. You can also use a alternate method of making T-shirts with the aid of your computer and printer. Check www.smartguypress.com, click on "Archives", then "April" and look for "Create Your Own Custom T-shirts".

Spreadsheets

A spreadsheet is a program that can manipulate numerical

181

data. The spreadsheet display is a matrix of "cells". Cells can contain numbers, formulas, or both. Most spreadsheet programs can generate charts and graphs from the data contained within its cells. Spreadsheets are very popular for computing financial information. Below is a screen shot of a spreadsheet designed to calculate and keep track of college income and expenses.

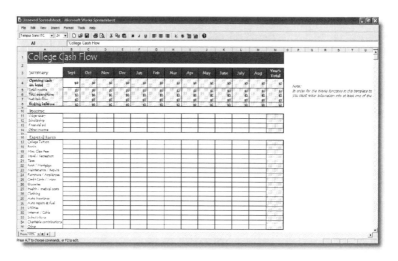

Databases

Database programs are used to store and manipulate large quantities of data. The data can be any kind. Most databases contain text or numerical information such as addresses, stock numbers, or recipes. Some databases though, hold graphics, frames of video or entire videos, and even music. The data in a database is stored in a record, and each record contains fields. If you're familiar with a box of recipe cards, then you know the basics of a database. The box itself would be the database. The individual cards are the records. Each unique piece of information on each card is a separate field.

182

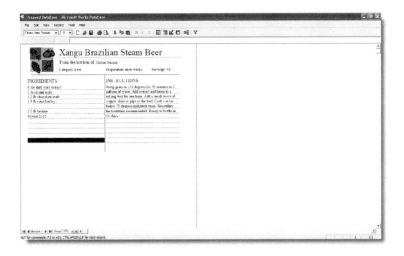

In the above recipe database, you see one record. The fields of the record are as follows: recipe name, author, preparation time, number of servings, ingredients and instructions.

What makes a database really useful is the ability to do searches on specific fields and create reports. For example, prior to a dinner party, you might search your recipe database for all soup recipes, with preparation times of less than three hours, and five or more servings.

In addition to recipes, many PC users use databases to hold the names and addresses of all their friends. This makes sending out Christmas or other holiday cards a snap. Once you find all the names and addresses you want to mail cards to, the program can then print them on adhesive labels or directly onto the envelopes.

Databases are also useful for creating form letters. You're familiar with form letters – you get them all the time in junk mail. They seem personalized, but they actually consist of some generic text with a few personalized fields from a database, such as your name and address. Most software "suites" and "works" programs (see explanation below) allow you to do this yourself. To do this you would set up a database of contact information, such as name, address – any fields you want. Then you create a generic document, and insert special placeholders for the field information. The final step is to perform a "mail merge" which takes field information from each record and inserts it into the generic document. Could be useful in writing relatives....

Suites and Works

Suites and Works, as in "Microsoft Office Suite" and "Microsoft Works", are combination programs which contain the most commonly used applications (word processor, database, spreadsheet, graphics presentation) in one bundle. The "suite" is more full-featured, and there is usually an upcharge to get it. The "suite" versions are popular with corporate America, though 90% of the features are never used.

Almost every PC sold today comes with the "works" version of either WordPerfect or Office included in the base price of the computer. These versions are perfectly usable and will satisfy 99.8% of new PC owners. Don't waste your money upgrading to the full version unless you absolutely have a need for it.[*]

Financial Programs

A great use for a PC is to keep and maintain your financial

---

[*] OpenOffice is a totally free application suite similar to Microsoft Office. I actually prefer it. Check this chapter for specifics. In fact, it would be a good idea to peruse the entire chapter before you purchase any software. You may be able to get what you need for free!

records. Several financial or bookkeeping applications exist, though the most popular for home use is Quicken, followed by Microsoft Money.

If you've ever wanted to get all your financial records in order, using your PC is definitely the way to do it. Unfortunately, if you already have trouble keeping your checkbook organized, using software isn't going to help.

If you want to take a stab at using your PC to maintain financial records without spending extra money, try using some of the provided financial templates included with Microsoft or Wordperfect Works.

Web Development

As you've just started your journey to PC proficiency, having your own website might seem like a flight of fancy. However, many ISP accounts come standard with a small web space, and creating your own website is really very easy.

Web pages are created primarily with a programming language known as "HTML". This is an acronym for "Hypertext Markup Language" and while it sounds exotic and complicated, it is really just a way of inserting codes into text to allow navigation with hyperlinks.

Before the Internet exploded in popularity, creating web pages, or HTML coding, was done manually using a word processor.

Today you can purchase several WYSIWYG or "drag and drop" Web applications. Microsoft Frontpage and Macromedia Dreamweaver are just two of several available.

To create simple web pages with Frontpage for example, you create, or insert text and graphics. You can edit the page directly in Frontpage in real-time. Once the page is completed to your taste, you upload the completed website to the web space you were provided by your ISP. This is very simple to do and a great way to share pictures with your friends and family.

Games

It's no secret that games (and porn) are the two biggest money makers in the PC world. To go further, I would say that the pace of hardware development is in large part due to the increased demands made by the latest games.

Games exist is every category you can think of and some are unbelievably realistic.

Along with the usual video games the kids love, such as role playing and shoot 'em up, there are lots of more traditional games, such as card and board games. Solitaire games are very popular. My Mom highly recommends Burning Monkeys Solitaire, which offers animated, joke telling-monkeys while you play. Check www.freeverse.com.

Internet games are also very popular now. I play online chess with people from all over the world. While there are some dedicated, full-featured Internet games which require a fee to play, such as Internet Chess Club or Everquest, you can find many free games, especially board and card games at www.yahoo.com, as well as other "portal" sites.*

* A few years ago, online "portals" were the next big thing. Essentially, these were websites that offered many amenities that the average web surfer would find useful such as free e-mail, games, search engine, and news. This business model derived its revenue by selling

CD/DVD Burning

A relatively recent addition to the world of personal computers, CD/DVD drives that write to a disk have become extremely popular.

CD/DVD drives are optical, as opposed to magnetic drives like hard and floppy disks. Writing to an optical drive is often referred to as "burning". This requires a specific type of drive and admittedly, this is a confusing area. Seriously, I won't even attempt to explain in detail all the various acronyms and formats.

Whatever type of drive your PC came with is most likely supported by an included application – in addition to the built-in CD burning feature of Windows XP. Check the documentation that came with your PC.

TOP SECRET The one thing you do need to understand about CD/DVD drives, no matter which type you have, is that they are just another form of storage, much like a hard disk. They are simply another, and in this case removable and easily transported, place to store files. Many newbies are under the impression that if a computer has a DVD drive capable of writing to a disk (not all can), they can make copies of commercial DVD movies and/or create videos that will play on a standard DVD player. Copies of commercial DVDs can be made, but this requires additional software and is illegal. Creating movies that play on standard DVD players can also be done, but will require additional software as well. Just keep in mind that just because you have a video, slide show, or

advertisements. Many subsequently failed.

presentation that plays on your computer, you cannot simply save it to a **DVD** disk and expect it to play on a standard **DVD** player. I am calling special attention to this as I've recently run into a number of people who thought they could copy a **Powerpoint** presentation or a slide show on to a **DVD** and have it play on a standard **DVD** player. Not so...

Messengers and Chat

Instant messenger programs provide a means of chatting, via text, over the Internet in real-time. Several different types are available, with the most popular being Yahoo and AOL. Both of these are free – you just download the application, called a client, and register for an account.

These programs are particularly popular with teenagers who will happily wile away the hours chatting, (called "im'ing" by the younger set) with friends.

TOP SECRET To talk to your family and friends through an instant messenger you'll need to download and install the client, if it isn't already. You'll also need to register online for the service, exchange screen names with your friends and family, and make sure that you are both using the same **IM** client.

Instant messaging programs also allow access to the infamous chat rooms you occasionally hear about on the news. The story usually revolving around an adult trying to solicit a child for sex. Don't get the idea that chatting on the Internet is the root of all evil, but there are dangers to be aware of and I highly recommend supervising youngsters when they are online.

Another type of Internet chatting, which offers both real-time messaging and chat rooms is IRC – Internet Relay Chat. IRC is actually a chat protocol established in 1988, and in the computer world, that is ancient.

Similar to instant messenger clients, to use IRC you'll need an IRC client, such as mIRC. You then log on to one of many available servers and choose a nickname. You can then choose a chat room from a displayed list.

In addition to chatting, IRC is also a haven for "file traders" – people who use the Internet to trade different types of files, usually illegal (copyrighted) music, video, or pornography.

If you're looking to chat in real-time over the Internet, instant messaging is your best option – it's free, and easy to get started.

IRC is a viable option, especially if you have a desire to increase your video or music collection. However, IRC is difficult to use and quite risky if you don't know what you're doing.

TOP SECRET If you've chosen for some reason to use AOL as your ISP, you'll need to be concerned about instant messages. By default, AOL instant messenger is installed along with the AOL client. So if you are on AOL, you're already set up to instant message. This is obviously a good thing if you're looking to chat. However, many, many new AOL users have been frightened, and in many cases duped, by con men using instant messenger. Whenever you are online through AOL, people can send you an instant message. When they do this, a window pops up on screen accompanied by a sound. This can be very startling to someone not expecting it, and even worse if they don't have any idea what it is.

In addition, unscrupulous con men and pranksters send out thousands of messages saying something along the lines of "This is an AOL administrator and we need you to input your password to continue online". People who have no idea what an instant message even is, and many AOL users are computer newbies, will often type in their password. This, of course, gives complete control of the AOL account to the hacker. Bottom line: Never give your password to anyone or anything after you have already logged on. If in doubt, log off and call your ISP on the phone. See Chapter 10 for more about online security.

Graphics and Paint

As described in Chapter 5, graphics programs can be used to display (open) image files. In addition, these applications can be used to create or alter images.

Certainly the most common usage for these applications is manipulating pictures taken with a digital camera. For example, you could remove the "red-eye" from pictures of your pets.

If you have recently purchased a new PC, chances are good that you already have a basic graphics program installed. Look for Adobe Photoshop Album or Microsoft Image Composer as these are most likely included with "shovelware".*

---

* "Shovelware" refers to all of the software, much of it of questionable quality, included with new PCs.

The most popular image applications are Adobe Photoshop and Paintshop Pro.

Drafting

When I was in school, drafting class consisted of drawing geometric shapes using plastic triangles and T-squares. The drawings were time-consuming, and if you made a mistake, get out the eraser.

Today, all of that has been replaced by computers and CAD (computer-aided drafting) programs. These programs create dimensioned drawings and can be changed and resized with the click of a mouse.

CAD is definitely a specialized application and the learning curve can be quite steep, particularly if you are not familiar with traditional drafting. However, if you have a need for dimensioned drawings, this is the way to go.

TOP SECRET **If you've read the previous chapters dealing with interaction, navigation and files, and application basics, you should have no trouble learning new applications. Start with a word processor. Create a few documents of various types. Remember to consult the application's online help or the printed documentation (if it came with any) if you run into any problems. Once you really start to understand how software works, learning new applications is relatively easy as they have many things in common.**

Here is a great tip to keep in mind if you're stuck: Most applications are based on the create, select, then modify concept. What this means is that you will usually create whatever data (text, graphics, numbers in spreadsheets),

then select the parts you want to change and modify them using tools and commands. If a tool or command is not working, ask yourself "Do I need to select something first?". Many times this is the problem.

And don't forget the value of experimenting. Try all the various tools and menu commands and see what happens!

Shareware and Freeware

The above sections describe various types of software applications. Most new computer users assume that to obtain software you need to purchase it from a store. For most commercial software this is true.

However, other types of software that are either free or available for a small fee exist. This shareware/freeware as it is called, can be of surprisingly high-quality. In fact, I rarely purchase commercial software and when I do, it is only after I have conducted a thorough search for a shareware or freeware alternative that can meet my needs. If none exist, I may choose to go the commercial route. Check the chart below for specific differences between software types.

Type of Software	Cost	Copyright?	Where to obtain
Commercial	Expensive – $10 -$1000s	Yes, cannot distribute legally	Computer and electronic stores; many online vendors
Shareware	Low – most $10-$50	Yes, usually encourages distribution	Online
Freeware	None – Free!	Yes, but free to distribute	Online
Public-Domain	None – Free!	No, can be distributed and even modified	Online

I mention a few of my favorite shareware/freeware applications in Chapter 10. You can also find a plethora of information, including reviews, online.

OpenOffice

As I mentioned briefly, OpenOffice (www.openoffice.org) is a free application suite that is in many ways comparable to Microsoft Word or Wordperfect Suite, both of which cost several hundred dollars.

OpenOffice includes a full-featured word processor, spreadsheet, database, drawing and multi-media program. I love OpenOffice, and have used it exclusively for writing – including creating and editing this very book.

Before you shell out your hard earned cash on a commercial product, give OpenOffice a try and see if it fits your needs. Though the program is absolutely free, if you like it as much as I think you will, consider making a donation at www.openoffice.com to help fund future development.

Chapter 9

Help It's Broke!

Read carefully – I am about to save you a bunch of money. Really. If you visit a local "big box" PC retailer, such as Best Buy, Circuit City, or CompUSA, you'll see several people milling around the technical support desk waiting to get their PCs repaired. The information contained in this chapter will prevent you from having to make that trip. In fact, the technicians at these stores use exactly the same procedures I am about to teach you.

Without a doubt, something on your PC, be it hardware or software, is going to break at some point. Unfortunately, this is just the way it is. And most likely, it is going to occur just when you need to send an urgent e-mail or print an important document.

However, there are several simple things you can do that will "fix" the majority of common problems. Also, there are several things you can do to prevent problems from occurring in the first place.

The most common problems include:

- **Freezing** – Certain portions of the computer lock-up and refuse to work. Sometimes everything freezes; all programs and Windows. Other times, it may be just one program or even part of a program. With time, you'll come to know when your PC is experiencing this phenomenon. When you're just starting out though, give your PC a minute or two before attempting the troubleshooting steps below. Not everything with computers takes place instantaneously. What you think may be a freeze might just be the PC taking some time to calculate the task at hand. This is especially true if the hard disk activity status light is blinking. Reading from and writing to a disk can take some time.

- **Crashing** – Computer software can crash. That is, for whatever reason, the computer and software become very confused. When this happens the software says "I am outta here!" and quits. Windows then displays a dialog box telling you that the program suffered an "unexpected error". Which begs the question "Are there expected errors?" Generally when a crash occurs, you will lose your unsaved work, but can restart the application and continue working. Occasionally if Windows itself gets really confused, you may encounter the "blue screen of death". The screen goes blue and some unintelligible error messages are displayed. Normally this will require a hard reset. (See section on rebooting below)

- **Internet Connectivity Problems** – The computer and software seem to be working properly, but you can't connect to the Internet. Usually, if everything else is functioning properly and nothing has changed since the last time your connection worked, the problem will be your ISP and not your computer or software. In this case, note which status lights on your modem are lit and call your ISP.

- **Won't Boot** – You power on the computer and nothing happens or the boot process appears to hang and never complete. With past versions of Windows, this was a relatively common occurrence. One of XP's best new features has drastically reduced this issue however. System File Protection automatically, without you ever knowing it, maintains and even replaces critical system files if they become damaged, deleted, or overwritten. Still, on certain days, the computer gods will smite you with a non-booting PC. This can usually be resolved by restarting in "Safe Mode" and using "System Restore" to turn back time.

TOP SECRET You attempt to power on your PC and are greeted with the ominous message: *"Invalid system disk (or Non-system disk); Replace and strike any key when ready"*. **"What is going on?" you ask. This is Microsoft's, er, technospeak for "You probably left a floppy disk in the floppy drive. Take it out and press any key to continue." When a PC attempts to boot, it looks at various disk drives for a suitable Operating System (OS). Normally, it will first check the floppy drive, then the hard disk and finally the CD-ROM drive. If it looks at the floppy drive and finds a disk without a suitable OS, it freaks out and displays the above message. If there is no floppy disk in the drive and you still get the above message, this is known in the biz as "a very bad thing". It means that the PC cannot find a suitable OS on any disk. In this thankfully rare case, you may have to reinstall the OS from the CDs included with your PC.**

If you encounter a problem with something that previously worked, follow these steps to rectify the problem:

1. **Save all open files**. If possible, save all open files and close all applications. If your mouse is frozen, or items on the screen are unavailable, this may not be possible.

2. **Reboot the PC**. Computers are complex systems of hardware and software and occasionally, for lack of a better phrase, things get out of whack. Rebooting the PC resolves many issues and should be your first course of

action when something that previously worked stops working. If a reboot doesn't resolve the problem, go to the next step.

3. **Ask yourself "What has changed?"** Have you installed any software or made any control panel or preference changes that could account for the problem you're experiencing? If so, you may want to try reversing those changes to see if that resolves the issue. This is known in the industry as "backing out" your changes. In the corporate IT world, this is a daily occurrence.

4. **Use "System Restore".** This allows you to "roll-back" your computer to an earlier time when it did function properly.

Rebooting

Rebooting, also known as "restarting", solves many problems by clearing memory and killing lingering processes.

To reboot:

1. Click on **Start→ Turn Off Computer**. A dialog box is displayed with "Standby", "Turn Off", and "Restart" buttons".

2. Click once on "**Restart**". Windows shuts down and then restarts automatically.

3. Log back on and verify that the problem has been resolved.

Occasionally, you'll experience a problem that will prevent you from using the above method to reboot. The mouse may "freeze" onscreen or the Start menu may not function. Whatever the reason, if you cannot use the above method to reboot, you must perform a "hard reset".

A "hard reset" essentially removes power from the computer and forces it to shut down. The power button is then pressed again to restart the computer. There are times when this is required, though you don't want to perform this procedure in place of a normal shutdown as it doesn't allow Windows to finish writing to the hard disk. A power interruption while a disk is writing (saving) can lose data, or in some very rare cases, damage the disk.

To force a shut down (hard reset):

1. **Hold down the computer's power button until the status light goes out.** This usually takes 5-10 seconds

2. **Press the power button again to restart the computer.**

TOP SECRET If a program you're using suddenly freezes (stops responding), you can attempt to kill just that program. This may allow you to carry on with your work in other open programs without restarting your computer. To do this, hold down the ctrl and alt keys and press the delete key once. Pressing twice or holding down delete may reboot the system. Ctrl+alt+delete will display the following dialog box.

Select the program that is frozen and click the "End Task" button. You may or may not get a box telling you that the program is waiting for something and asking if you'd like to wait. Decline the courtesy and kill it immediately.

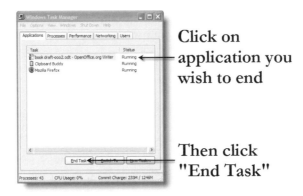

Click on
application you
wish to end

Then click
"End Task"

Note the additional tabs across the top of the task manager. Feel free to select these tabs. There is some interesting information contained within.

TOP SECRET Computers don't behave like other electrical devices, such as VCRs, DVD players, or hair dryers. The are not "instant-on" and "instant-off". They require time to boot (start) and time to shutdown. They also differ in that you can safely leave a PC powered on for days, weeks, months or even years! This will not cause any problems. No explosions, no fires, no damage. This allows for instant access to the computer. It is a good idea however, to reboot (restart) the computer occasionally to prevent memory leaks and errors from occurring. Also, if you're using a CRT display, turn it off when you're not using your system to save energy and prevent image burn-in from occurring. This is a phenomenon where a ghost-like image becomes permanently burned into the screen after days of displaying the same image. This used to be a fairly common occurrence, but technological progress has largely made this a thing of the past. Screen savers, programs that display a moving image after a period of

inactivity, were originally developed to prevent burn-in from occurring

System Restore

If a reboot doesn't fix your problem, the next step is to try System Restore – the big gun of Window's administration tools.

I am not a big fan of Microsoft products. From my experience, they tend to be enormous bloated blobs of errors, inconsistencies, and security holes. I am also not fond of "features" which attempt to show or hide items based on how often you view them. Microsoft also has a reputation for, um, let's just say "borrowing" others' ideas. Multiple lawsuits, including some judgments against them for dubious business practices have occurred in the last several years.

Occasionally, they get it right though. Windows XP is a huge improvement over previous generations in terms of features, compatibility, and rock-solid stability.

TOP SECRET **If something that previously worked stops working, ask yourself "What changed"? Rarely, if ever, does something spontaneously stop working. There is usually a definitive reason, and almost always it's due to a change.**

One feature that Microsoft got *really* right is System Restore. System Restore is built in to Windows XP. In essence, it allows you to "roll back" the hard disk on your computer to an earlier time – a time when everything was working properly.

System Restore accomplishes this by creating "System

Restore points". For example, say you install a new program and as it turns out, it won't run. In addition, some of your other programs have stopped functioning properly since the install. You could go to the add/remove programs control panel and try to remove the newly installed application. However, poorly designed and coded applications are not likely to have the best installer routines. Many "reinstalls" leave a trail of files and registry entries – useless gunk – after they have completed. So, you use System Restore to roll back your hard disk to a time right before you did the install of the ill-behaving program.*

This is a fantastic feature that up until XP came out, was only available by purchasing a third-party application.

However, there are of course a few interesting details to know before you begin to assume that your PC is goof proof.

First, System Restore does *not* restore any files stored in the "My Documents" folder or any of its sub folders. Microsoft's documentation claims that this "protects your personal files". I guess you might find that accurate unless a personal file is what you're trying to restore! Now, it is not very likely that you would want System Restore to bring back personal files, but it is possible that a situation could occur when you wish it would. Microsoft should make it an option in future releases.

Second, you obviously have to have a restore point to roll back to. Windows XP creates several different restore points automatically:

---

* The "registry" is Window's internal database. It contains an enormous amount of settings in records called "registry entries". Windows experts occasionally change these entries manually to hack – customize – their system.

- **Initial System Checkpoint** – The date and time the computer was first used if it came preinstalled with Windows XP. If upgrading to XP, it will be from the date and time of the initial install. This *could* be very useful. Over time as unused files, Registry entries, and other gunk build up on your hard disk, Windows may slow down or become flaky. In the biz, this is known as "software rot". The absolute fix for this used to be backing up all user data, formatting (erasing) the hard disk, re-installing Windows and finally re-installing the applications and user data. With System Restore, you simply go back to the Initial System Checkpoint. You'll still have to re-install any applications you installed after that, but that's not always a bad thing. This is the perfect opportunity for a bit of housecleaning. This means only installing what you really need. As I said this *could* be very useful, however System Restore *deletes* restore points after 90 days!

- **System Restore points** – System Restore automatically creates restore points. It does this every 24 hours of calendar time or every 10 hours of computer up time. These can certainly be useful.

- **Program Install Points** – Often when computers break, it occurs right after a new program is installed. The offending program installs a bad .dll file or a different version of DirectX and things go bad. System Restore creates automatic restore points before installing new programs whenever Installshield or XP installer are used for the install. Most installs do use one of these, but be safe and create a manual restore point (see below) before installing any new software.

- **Windows XP Auto Update Points** – Windows XP can be configured to automatically check for OS updates via

203

the Internet. If this is turned on, System Restore will create a checkpoint before installing any update. This is a good thing. Though once you become familiar with XP you may want to turn off auto updates and initiate them manually. It's not really a problem to leave auto update turned on, but it will pop up an annoying text balloon frequently informing you that updates are ready.

In addition to automatically created restore points, you can create a manual restore point at any time. To do this:

1. Select **Start→help and support**

2. Then click either on the System Recovery icon or the System Restore hypertext under "See Also".

3. At the System Restore wizard, click "Create a System Restore point", then "Next" and enter a relevant name. Something like "Before install of Microsoft office". The wizard will automatically provide a time and date stamp.

You should manually create a restore point before installing programs, adding hardware or trying anything risky, such as editing system files or the Registry. Both of which are advanced topics not covered in this book and really not necessary for the average PC user.

To restore your PC to a previous time when everything was working properly:

1. **Start→All Programs → Accessories → System Tools → System Restore**. You can also access System Restore from **Start→Help and Support**

2. Click the "**Restore my computer to an earlier time**"

radio button and then click "**Next**".

3. The days of the calendar in bold have restore points associated with them. Click a day in bold to display a list of restore points. Then click the restore point you wish to use. Click "**Next**".

4. Click "**Next**" again and the PC will gather needed information, then reboot and roll-back the hard disk to the earlier time. When the log-in screen appears, it is finished.

5. You can always "undo" the above restore by following the same steps and selecting "**Undo my last restoration**".

Safe-Mode

As mentioned in the beginning of this chapter, occasionally PCs simply refuse to boot. This is a bad thing as there is no way to use System Restore if the PC won't boot...or is there?

Safe-mode is a special stripped-down, bare-bones version of Windows that loads and uses only what is absolutely necessary for Windows to operate. In many cases, a PC that will not boot will run just fine in safe-mode, thus allowing you to run System Restore and rewind your hard disk to an earlier time when everything was working.

So, if you PC will not boot, do the following:

1. Power on the PC.

2. This next step can be tricky timing-wise. As the computer attempts to boot, it may or may not display diagnostic messages. This will depend on the brand of PC. Immediately after the messages end, repeatedly tap the F8

key. If messages are not displayed, start tapping the F8 key. If you tap too early, or too frequently, you will get a "Keyboard Error" message. If this happens, restart the computer and try again. The key is to be tapping the F8 key just before the first Windows screen appears. When you get the timing just right, the Windows Advanced Options menu screen will appear.

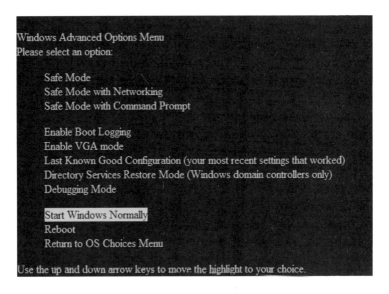

3. Use the arrow keys to move the selection to "**Safe Mode**" and press the "**Enter**" key. If at any time you are asked to select an Operating System, select Windows XP and press "**Enter**". Diagnostic text will scroll down the screen and eventually you'll be presented with a login window.

4. Log in as normal. You'll get a message box informing you that you're in safe mode. This is hardly necessary as you'll quickly notice that the Desktop, icons, and menus appear to be drawn by crack-addled hieroglyphic painters. That's because in safe mode, Windows doesn't load drivers for

specific hardware, such as your video card. It loads generic drivers that work with all hardware in case the drivers are what is causing the boot problems.*

5. Refer to the earlier instructions and run System Restore to rewind your hard disk to an earlier time.

Preventing Problems

The ideal situation is to prevent problems from ever occurring in the first place. Some things you can do:

● Install the latest versions of programs and check for updates and patches frequently. This applies to Windows XP itself also.

● Use a personal firewall. ZoneAlarm from Zone Labs works great and they offer a totally free version. It's all you'll need.

● Use virus protection. I recommend another free product; AVG Anti-Virus available at www.grisoft.com. This is a great, full-featured product that does exactly what you need it to do.

● Ditch Microsoft Internet Explorer and use the FireFox browser. IE is buggy, full of security holes, and has more patches issued for it than any other application I can think of. Use FireFox and eliminate a host of security threats, annoying pop-ups, and spyware. An awesome program and again, totally free. Although I do recommend giving a donation or at least buying a T-shirt.

---

* "Drivers" are small applications – software – used by the OS to control specific hardware such as video and sound cards.

Installing and using ZoneAlarm, FireFox, and AVG Anti-Virus are covered in detail in Chapter 10.

Learn by Destruction!

After a particularly exasperating computer session, my mom likes to call and ask "How did you ever learn all this stuff"? The answer is really not a big mystery. I did research, a considerable amount of reading, and lots of trial and error.

Put another way, I would try different things just to see what would happen and if something broke in the process, well, I would learn a lot by fixing it. And in those days, we didn't have System Restore....

TOP SECRET Reading will get you a long way when using a PC. Carefully reading online help, web pages, and books will allow you to solve any issue you might encounter.

You probably know a young child who is very proficient using a PC. How do kids catch on to all this new technology so quickly? Some of this knowledge flows via word of mouth. Much of it though, is the result of simply trying different things and figuring out what works. Kids, unlike many adults, don't usually have the fear of breaking the computer.

System Restore should relieve you of all your fears of hurting the computer. If you are someone who is concerned about breaking their new computer, create a restore point manually each time you begin a computing session. This way, you can always return to a time when your system was functioning properly and never have to worry about "doing something wrong".

Getting Technical Support

Occasionally, no matter what preventative measures you've taken or what fixative solutions you've tried, something will break and you'll have no choice but to ask for assistance. That assistance might be from the company that makes the product, a hired technician, or even a tech savvy friend or family member.

Regardless of the source, getting the help you need can be a frustrating and annoying experience. It doesn't have to be though. Here are a few things to keep in mind when seeking outside help for a PC problem:

● Write down the problem you're having before talking to anyone. Be as specific and precise as possible.

● If the problem is associated with an error message or other on-screen text, write down the exact message. Details count!

● Make note of exactly what you were doing before the problem occurred.

With all of the information assembled, it is much easier to converse with a technician and resolve your problem quickly.

Technical support analysts, the people you talk to when you call tech support, have a tough, thankless job. The people who call technical support are often frustrated and angry. Remain calm while talking to tech support. They are there to help you as quickly as possible.

After you describe your problem, the tech support person

will most likely instruct you to try some things to resolve your issue. Follow their instructions to the letter. If you don't understand what they are saying, ask for step-by-step instructions.

Chapter 10

Adware, Spyware, and Internet Security

Malware

How times change. Just like having sex, using a PC connected to the Internet used to be fun and low risk. Today though, there are thousands of bugs, viruses, trojans, adbots, spyware, pop-ups and other software nasties just waiting to turn your PC into someone else's robot, or worse, a completely unusable zombie.

These types of malicious software (hence the name, malware) come in many forms.

- **Viruses** – These are small applications that are typically disguised as something useful, or at least benign. When the virus program is run, it attempts to replicate itself and infect other connected computers. It also may do things like erase files or spawn looping processes that can crash a PC. Viruses are usually transmitted by e-mail in the form of attachments.

- **Trojans** – These are small applications usually disguised as something useful. Unlike viruses though, their main objective is not to replicate but to install in a way that they always start when you turn on your PC. What they do after it starts varies, though they are usually destructive in nature. A very common trait of trojans is to open a "backdoor". This backdoor allows a knowledgeable hacker to take control of your PC. Obviously, this is a very bad thing. Trojans are usually contracted by downloaded software or by e-mail attachments.

- **Spyware/Adbots** – Currently spyware is the biggest malware problem. Developing programs and methods to fight spyware has become a multi-million dollar industry. These usually unseen programs install themselves in your system surreptitiously. Once there, they collect and transmit data, such as surfing habits, passwords and other personal information. Some sources are estimating that over 85% of all PCs are infected with spyware. Spyware is usually contracted when installing downloaded software. However, it can also be contracted through inherent flaws in some web browsers, most notably Internet Explorer.

- **Homepage Hijackers** – All browsers allow the user to set their homepage to whatever page they would like. I personally have mine set to www.excite.com, which offers a personalized news and e-mail page. Homepage hijackers take advantage of a flaw in some browsers (notably Microsoft Internet Explorer again....you might be starting to see a pattern) to set your homepage to something you definitely don't want, like a porn or advertising site – in some cases, permanently. Homepage hijackers are usually contracted when visiting websites that take advantage of flaws and security holes in web browsers.

- **Spam** – Spam refers to all the garbage e-mail that you'll receive as soon as you set up an e-mail account. These range from simple advertising of useless and pornographic products to outright scams and cons.

- **Pop-ups** – Pop-ups are usually associated with web browsing, though some trojans display pop-ups even when you're not using a browser. Pop-ups while browsing are a problem as they obscure the screen, display inappropriate material, and even crash your computer if enough pop-ups are displayed. Not all pop-us are malevolent however.

Some reputable websites utilize pop-ups, though their use is declining as more "pop-up blocker" utilities are being developed. Personally, I hate pop-ups, and refuse to use them when designing web pages.

Luckily, with just a small amount of forethought and preparation, all of these Internet nasties can be fixed and more importantly, prevented from occurring in the first place. Follow the tips below and you won't have to worry about these kind of security threats. Ignore them and you will be infected – guaranteed.

Oh, like the previous chapter, the info contained here will also save you a ton of money. Skeptical? Take another trip down to your local "big-box" computer retailer. This time, take a walk over to the software isle, specifically the section where anti-spyware and anti-virus programs are displayed. Chances are this will be one of the more busy areas of the store.... Fortunately, you won't be purchasing any of these programs. Just follow the directions below.

Install and Use an Anti-Virus Program

There was a time when a virus protection program was an option. No longer is that the case. You must install, use and continuously upgrade a virus protection program to prevent infection.

I am not a fan of most commercial Anti-Virus programs, such as Norton Anti-Virus and McCaffee. It seems to me there is a potential conflict of interest when a company's revenue is based on selling upgrades to combat new viruses. Is it such a leap to think that these same companies might be creating new viruses just to sell additional upgrades? Maybe it is just my conspiratorial mindset....

Anyway, I've mostly used free Anti-Virus software and have had great success. Currently I am using AVG Anti-Virus. It is available for free, download it at www.grisoft.com.

Sadly, if you've recently purchased a new PC ,chances are it already has a commercial Anti-Virus product installed. These are usually "trial" versions that expire within a few months and require you to pay a fee if you wish to keep using them.

If this situation applies to you, use the PC as it came from the factory. By the time the trial version expires you'll be able to download and install AVG Anti-Virus yourself, thus saving you hundreds of dollars.

Install and Use a Firewall

A firewall is a software application that runs in the background and controls all of the network or Internet activity both in and out of a computer. A firewall can be configured to limit certain types of access, thus protecting your computer from hackers and potential security risks. In addition, a firewall can alert you or create a log of all activity, some of which is easily identifiable as trojans or spyware attempting to access the Internet. Firewalls are especially important if you are connected to the Internet via a broadband connection.

Windows XP has an integral firewall, though it is very limited in features. If you're just starting out, you can certainly use this firewall. However, as soon as you're relatively comfortable using your PC I highly recommend using a different firewall. One of the most popular, as well as being free, is ZoneAlarm by ZoneLabs.

You can download ZoneAlarm from www.zonelabs.com.

They offer a few different versions, but for the majority of home users the free version is totally adequate and vastly superior to the firewall included with Windows.

Install and Use FireFox

As mentioned several times throughout the book, I am a big fan of the FireFox web browser. It is extremely easy to use, very stable, fast, and perhaps most importantly, is very secure. FireFox has built-in pop-up protection that actually works and is immune to most, if not all, of the security exploits used against Internet Explorer. Oh, and did I mention that FireFox is totally free? I highly recommend downloading, installing, and using FireFox as soon as you get online.

To download and install FireFox:

1. Open your current browser. (This is probably Internet Explorer)

2. Enter the web address (URL) "www.getfirefox.com" and press the enter key.

Click to start download

3. After the web page loads, click on "**Free Download**" in the upper right corner.

4. A dialog box appears asking what to do with the file you're downloading. Click "**Save**". A file save dialog box appears.

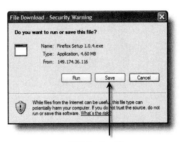

Click Save

5. Using your recently acquired expertise in files and navigation, select the location where the downloaded file will be saved and click the "**Save**" button. The choice, as always, is yours to make. Most downloaded applications (including FireFox) come in the form of an "installer program". The installer is runs and places the needed parts of the application where they need to go. Therefore, after installation you can safely discard the downloaded install program to avoid clutter and free up disk space. For this reason, I have created a "temp" folder on my Desktop for all my downloads. After I install the application, I simply drag the installer file to the trash.

6. After the download completes (how long it takes depends on the speed of your Internet connection), a "Download Complete" dialog box appears. Click "**Run**".

Click to start
installer

7. A "security warning" dialog box may or may not appear. If it does, click on "**Run**". The FireFox installer will appear.

8. Read the dialog box text and click "**Next**" as necessary.

9. You'll be asked to read and agree to the EULA, as well as the location that FireFox should be installed.* The default location (C:\Program Files\Mozilla FireFox) is fine.

10. Click "**Finish**" and FireFox is successfully installed.* Now, whenever you are connected to the Internet (with broadband you are always connected), simply run FireFox to browse the web. If you have

---

* EULA is an acronym for "End User License Agreement". Whenever you install software, the installer will display and want you to agree to the EULA. Generally, these texts limit the use of copying, etc. However, sometimes you are asked to agree to installing spyware or adware on your computer. While time consuming, I recommend reading the EULA whenever they are displayed.

* The above procedure is representative of how most software is installed.

additional questions though, surf over to www.getfirefox.com for complete documentation and tutorials.

Install and Use Spybot Search and Destroy

Spybot Search and Destroy is one of many programs available to detect and remove spyware from your system. SSD is technically a free program. However, the author requests donations if you like and use the program. I recommend donating. You can do this by credit card, using a link on the SSD site. If you are just getting started on the Internet, perhaps wait until you're more knowledgeable before entering your credit card number on any website. (See below)

The official website for SSD is http://www.safer-networking.org/en/home/index.html.

You can click on "download" at that site or surf to

www.download.com and enter "spybot search and destroy" in the search field. Then click on the "Spybot Search and Destroy" link to display the download page. Here you can read all the specifics of the program, including the download.com review (they gave it 5 out of 5). Next, click on "Download". A file save dialog box will display. Navigate to the location you'd like to save the SSD installer file. A temp folder you create on your Desktop is a suitable place.

When the download has finished, run the installer, and click "Next" as needed to complete the installation.

Using SSD is fairly intuitive, so feel free to run the application and play with all of its features. I highly recommend browsing the SSD website for tutorials, help files, and answers to frequently asked questions.

Usernames and Passwords

As mentioned in Chapter 5, once you get online you'll be deluged with usernames and passwords. You already have a username and password for your ISP account, and you'll need to create and use many others as you surf the Internet. Even some news websites are requiring users to register before they can browse the site. Of course you can always choose to frequent sites that don't require you to register.

Many websites you've probably at least heard of, such as Ebay and Amazon, require users to create accounts in order to actually use the website. If you just want to browse these sites, registration is not needed.

When creating usernames and passwords keep these things in mind:

- Make both usernames and passwords something easy to remember and meaningful to you, but not something that would be easy for others to guess.

- When creating passwords, consider using a "pass phrase". Simply think of a phrase that is meaningful and easy to remember, then use the first letter of each word as your password. For example, "my kids are named Neil and Amy and my dog is Buster" becomes "mkannaamadib".

- Add numbers to a password to make it even more difficult for someone to guess. For example "6mkannaamdib3".

- For websites where you have a credit card on file or other sites where you absolutely want to have a secure password, use the tips above along with random capitalization. For example "6mKaNnaamaDIb3".

- Be aware that some sites limit the length that a username or password can be to eight characters.

- Create a simple document in notepad or something similar, called "Online Accounts", and keep track of all your usernames and passwords. Print this document and file it somewhere safe so you have a hard copy. Be sure and update both copies whenever you add accounts or make changes.

- Some sites use your e-mail address in place of a username. You might want to create multiple e-mail addresses and use only one of those on commercial websites. Use something that has no real association with your real name for this particular e-mail address.

- Using the same usernames and passwords on multiple sites

obviously increases your risk. Using unique usernames and passwords at every different site increases your overall Internet security, though it increases the complexity of remembering them all. You may want to use the same username and password on sites that are low-risk, such as non-commercial sites, discussion groups, etc.

Miscellaneous Security Topics

Have you ever known someone who seemed like an intelligent person, but was continually involved in car accidents?

You'll find similar people who regularly have computer problems. Their computers are always the first to be infected with new viruses. They've had their credit card numbers stolen and used without their knowledge. And, increasingly, they've been the victims of the relatively new crime, identity theft.

Like the preceding car accident "victims", these computer "victims" are doing something wrong – in most cases, they're doing a lot of things wrong. Whether out driving a car, answering a phone call from a telemarketer or surfing the Internet, it is vitally important that you take precautions and remain vigilant at all times!

Crooks in large numbers have moved onto the Internet. There are countless numbers of cons, fakes, forgers and scams just waiting for an unsuspecting surfer – more often than not, a newbie. By following a few common-sense rules, you can avoid ever being flim-flammed on the 'Net.

E-mail is the Root of all Internet evil!

- Given the media reports and advertising hype from the Anti-Virus software companies, you might be under the impression that computer viruses swim around the Internet much like the sentinels in the Matrix movies, just waiting to infect your computer. The truth, however, is a bit different. Most computer virus infections are the result of human error – specifically the result of the computer owner's error!. **Viruses usually enter a computer via an e-mail attachment or a downloaded file**. A few of them enter through security flaws in browsers, e-mail programs, or even Windows itself, but if you keep your software updated this shouldn't be an issue. So, prevention is really easy if you think about it. Never open an e-mail unless you know who the e-mail came from – personally. I am serious about this. No matter how tempting the offer in the subject line, immediately delete all e-mails from senders you don't know. This simple action will make your computer more secure than most. When opening e-mail attachments (obviously sent from someone you know), check the file type of the attachment. If the file extension is ".exe", the attachment is an executable file and could contain a virus. Don't open it until you verify with the person who sent it that they intentionally attached an executable file. Honestly, I don't open any attachments unless the person has told me in advance that they are sending one and I know exactly what is coming.

- E-mail addresses are easily faked. Faking a web or e-mail address is called "spoofing". Don't be surprised to see e-mails from your own address! This is one of many clever ploys designed to get you to open the mail and/or attachment.

222

- The links contained in an e-mail are also easily faked. To persuade you to open e-mails and attachments, scammers must earn your trust. One way they attempt to do this is by making the e-mail appear as though it originated from somewhere you trust – your bank, ISP, broker or utility company. Some e-mails will appear to have a web link to a legitimate site. These e-mails typically request you follow the link and enter some personal information. This is known as "phishing". Don't do it! Any e-mail requesting information of any kind should be summarily deleted.

If it's not E-mail ,it's Downloaded Software!

Common sense should again guide you when downloading files. Know the type of file you're downloading and where you're downloading it from. Downloading files from reputable sites such as download.com, shouldn't be a problem. But even reputable sites get spoofed occasionally, and that is the reason you should always run Anti-Virus software.

- And again, make sure you read the EULA when installing downloaded software. Many programs, especially file-sharing programs, are now installing spyware/adware along with the application you actually want to install. Many other "utility" programs, such as weather and search utilities, also install spyware/adware. Read the EULA carefully. To be extra sure, do a search for the program you're planning to download. Just type "programname spyware" into Google. You can also check at www.spywareinfo.com.

Miscellaneous Security Tips - Think Before You Click!

- Protect your personal information like your life depends on it! Lots of websites have forms where you can register for mailing lists or contests. "Win a prize!! Click here!!!" I recommend *not* doing this. The more places you put your e-mail address, the more spam and garbage will fill up your mailbox. Never give your e-mail or home address unless the website is a reputable commercial site like Ebay or Amazon. Never, ever, for any reason, enter your social security number on a web page. If there is a valid reason for needing this number, and at the moment I really can't think of one, do it over the phone with you initiating the call. Protect your passwords too! A lot of people get scammed on AOL. They'll be surfing the web and a small box will pop-up on screen asking them to re-enter their password. This is nothing but an outright scam by someone using the AOL instant messenger service to take advantage of new users. I follow a simple rule when it comes to phone solicitors, junk mail and e-mail, or any other request: If I don't initiate the contact, I ignore it.

- As you gain more experience online, you may at some point want to make online purchases. There are good, genuine deals to be had on the Internet and I myself do quite a bit of shopping online. But you need to be smart about it. If you have multiple credit cards, use only one for all your online shopping. This way you will be better able to track any problems. Carefully check your bill as soon as it arrives.

TOP SECRET Although it will not guarantee 100% protection against Internet fraud, making sure that you are dealing with a secure website will go a long way towards protecting yourself. In fact, entering a credit card number into a secure website is probably safer than physically handing it to a wait person at a restaurant. How can you tell if the web page you're on is secure? There are two ways: The URL in the address bar of the browser will display "https:" instead of "http:", and a small icon of a closed lock will appear in the lower right corner of the browser window. If you're using FireFox (and you should be!)the address field will also change from white to yellow. Check *before* you enter your card number!*

Secure web pages show "https" instead of "http" in the address field

Lock icon indicates secure web page

- In addition to credit cards, PayPal is another way to pay for items and services online. PayPal is a secure service that enables anyone with an e-mail address to send or receive money through the Internet. PayPal also allows small businesses, such as the publisher of this book, SmartGuy Press, to take credit cards for online purchases. Many online merchants, such as Ebay and iTunes, take payments directly from PayPal in addition to taking credit cards.* To enable this, you would open an account with PayPal and make an initial deposit through a credit card or

---

* Surf over to www.paypal.com for an example of a secure page.

* Paypal is owned by Ebay.

by tying your PayPal account to a bank account. I highly recommend PayPal and use it myself. In addition, the PayPal website (www.paypal.com) has loads of useful information about e-commerce and making online purchases.

- Unless you live on a different planet or don't watch TV, you probably have at least heard of Ebay, the Internet auction site. On Ebay, you can bid on virtually anything you can think of. You might also be interested in selling things yourself. Ebay *can* be a source of incredible bargains. Unfortunately, Ebay is also the hangout of many cyber thieves and con artists. Before you get involved in Ebay, do your homework. Ebay and PayPal have lots of information on their websites. Read all you can. Consider buying a book on Ebay before you start buying or selling.

- Again, think *before* you click! Scurrilous web developers are constantly trying new things to get you to click on their links. In some cases the link may be just a way to get you to their website – a form of advertising really, but annoying nonetheless – or it could be something much more malicious. Take a good look at the following graphic from a website that sends free electronic e-mail greeting cards.

Fake
warning
box

Notice that on the right hand side is what appears to be a Windows warning dialog box urging the user to "Scan your computer for critical errors". In fact, this "warning box" is a cleverly disguised graphic located on a web page. (Notice that it appears inside the web browser window.) Clicking on this box takes you to a website where malicious spyware will be installed on your PC if you click the "Yes, scan "My Computer" button. So, how do you avoid this? By hovering your mouse over the fake "warning window" you'll see the status bar in the lower left of the browser window display a web address. This is your first indication that the "warning box" is a web link and not an actual Windows dialog box. Another indication is that the browser's Title Bar and the fake "warning window" Title Bar are both selected. Remember that only one window can be active at any time. Additionally, actual Windows dialog boxes will show as open programs on the Windows task bar normally located at the very bottom of your screen (unless you've manually moved it).

And finally, remember these two old adages when surfing the

227

Internet:

- If it sounds too good to be true, it probably is.

- Nothing in life is free.

Chapter 11

Step-By-Step for Common Tasks

Up until this point, this book has focused on the general concepts of using a PC. This is so you, the user, can apply the knowledge you've gained to accomplish any task you wish.

This chapter will deal with the step-by-step instructions for accomplishing common tasks, including those that most new users are interested in. Feel free to use this chapter as a reference, especially when you're just beginning to learn the PC.

Keep in mind that Microsoft seems to be on a mission to see how many ways each task can be achieved. I've listed the most common and I think, the easiest and most efficient way of completing each task, but other ways certainly exist.

With many computer books, you get the "how" involved with completing a certain task, but not necessarily the "why". In most cases, the "why" is glaringly obvious, but not always. Beginners especially might be asking themselves "Why would I want to move or copy a file?". In cases where it isn't obvious, I've included the "why"....

Menu commands are indicated by the following format: **menuname→menucommand**.

Turning on the PC

1. Press the power button. If you have a desktop PC this is usually located on the front of the tower. On a laptop, the power button may be almost anywhere, but it is usually

above the keyboard. The symbol on most power buttons is a circle with a vertical line.

2. Turn on the monitor. This is usually a separate button on the monitor itself.

3. Wait for Windows to finish loading.

Turning off the PC

1. Start→Turn off computer→Turn off

2. Click the appropriate button:

Restart – Turns off computer and then reboots immediately

Turn off – Shuts the computer down completely.

Standby – Puts the computer in a state of sleep.

If the computer is "frozen", that is it won't turn off by performing the procedure above, you must do a "hard shutdown". Press and hold the power button for 10 seconds. I've had a few people tell me that even this procedure won't kill their PC. Remember, you can always unplug the PC from the wall.

Changing the Desktop Background

1. Right-click anywhere on the **Desktop**.

2. Select **Properties.**

3. Click the **Desktop** tab.

4. Choose from the list and click on **OK**. To use a graphic file of your own, click the **Browse** button and navigate to the file. Select the file, then click **Open**. Click **OK** to complete.

There are at least two other ways you can select a picture as your Desktop background, (also known as "wallpaper"):

● Double-click on the picture so it opens with Windows Picture and Fax Viewer. Then, right-click on the picture and select "**Set as Desktop Background**" from the context menu.

● Navigate to the file. Make sure **Thumbnails** is selected under the **View** menu. This makes picture files use their contents for display in the folder instead of icons. Right-click on the file and select "Set as Desktop Background" from the context menu. You must be in **Thumbnail** or **Filmstrip** view for the **Set as Desktop Background** menu item to be available.

You can also make changes here for screen saver and other appearance-related items. Feel free to play around with these.

Why do this? To adorn your screen with the picture of your choice. This is totally optional.

231

TOP SECRET The above process is for using a photo that you already have on your hard drive – either you downloaded it or imported it from a digital camera.

While surfing the web though, you might come across a cool picture you'd like to use as your Desktop wallpaper. Right-click on the image and select "Set as wallpaper" from the context menu. That's it! You may have to change the display properties for wallpaper to "Center" so that the image will display without distortion.

Change the Time or Date

1. Click twice on the actual time located at the right end of the Task Bar.

2. The date and time properties dialog box is displayed.

3. Change whatever setting you wish and click **OK**.

Note that checking the box under the **Internet Time** tab labeled "**Automatically sync with an Internet time server**" will allow Windows to maintain the correct time by automatically connecting to an accurate clock and syncing it with your PC. The only reason not to check this box is if you use a dial-up Internet connection.

Change Volume or Mute Sounds

1. Click once on the **speaker icon** located in the System Tray. The icon may be hidden. If it is, click once on the left arrow to display all System Tray icons. Oops! I mean "Notification Area" icons. Holding your mouse over an icon will display a text box (tooltip) with the icon's name.

2. Click and hold the left mouse button on the slider bar. Drag it wherever you want. Up is louder, down is quieter.

3. Click in the box next to **Mute** to turn off all sounds.

4. Click anywhere outside of the volume control itself to make it go away.

Start an Application

1. Start → All Programs → programfolder → programname

   Or

2. Double-click on the application icon or its shortcut wherever it is located, such as the Desktop or within a Desktop window.

Why do this? To start an application in order to write a letter, browse a website, play a game, etc.

See all the Files on your Hard Disk

1. Right-click on **Start.**

2. Select **Explore**.

Why do this? To find, move, or copy a file.

Navigate to a File

Several times in this book I've mentioned "navigate to a file". There are multiple ways to do this. The first one being the procedure outlined above in "See all the files on your hard disk". Here are a few other ways:

- Select **My Documents** from the **Start** menu and drill down through folders as needed.

- Select **My Pictures** from the **Start** menu and drill down through folders as needed.

- Select **My Music** from the **Start** menu and drill down through folders as needed.

- Select **My Computer** from the **Start** menu and drill down through folders as needed.

- Double-click on the **My Computer** icon if it is on your **Desktop**, drill down through folders as needed.

- Press ⊞ key + e to display **My Computer** in Explorer and drill down through folders as needed.

Select a File or Files

1. To select a file, left-click once on its icon. The icon darkens to indicate it is selected.

Most manipulation, such as copying, moving, and deleting files, can be done on individual files or multiple files at the same time. For example, you may want to move several files at once. For this, you'll need to select more than one file at a time. This is called "extended selection" and there are multiple ways to accomplish it.

1. Click on a file icon, hold down the ctrl key and click on another file icon.

2. Continue to hold down the ctrl key and click on additional icons as needed.

Another way:

1. To select all files that are in a contiguous block, that is, the files are next to each other. Click the first icon, hold down the shift key, and then click the last icon. All icons in between will become selected.

Another way:

1. Left-click and drag next to the files you want to select.

2. Any icon that the selection rectangle touches will become selected.

3. To select multiple groups of files that are not located near each other, hold down the shift key . So, drag a selection rectangle around the first group of files you wish to select. Then, hold down the shift key and select another group of files. The second group becomes selected as well as the first group. Hold down the shift key to select additional groups of files.

Copy a File

1. Navigate to the file you want to copy, either through Explorer or by clicking and drilling down through folders in Explorer windows.

2. Right-click on the file you want to copy and select **Copy** from the menu.

3. Navigate to the location you want to place the copy of the file.

4. Right-click in a blank area and select **Paste** from the

menu. Note that if you try to paste the copy in the same location (folder) the original file is located, it will have the words "Copy of" added before its filename.

To copy more than one file at a time, use extended selection (discussed in the previous section) first.

Why do this? Make a backup of an important file. Create a copy to modify so you don't ruin the original. Move a copy onto another disk for backup or for transfer to another PC.

Move a File

1. Navigate to the file you want to move, either through Explorer or by clicking and drilling down through folders in Explorer windows.

2. Right-click the file you want to move and select **Cut** from the menu. The icon of the "cut" file now appears ghosted – it won't fully disappear until you paste it somewhere else.

3. Navigate to the location you want to move the file to.

4. Right-click in a blank area and select **Paste** from the menu.

To move more than one file at a time, use extended selection first (see "select a File or Files" above).

Why do this? To organize your files by placing similar files in a common folder. For easier access, perhaps moving the file to the Desktop. To move files to the Recycling Bin.

Rename a File

1. Select the file you want to rename by clicking on it once.

2. Click one more time on the file name.

3. The name becomes highlighted. Type whatever name you'd like.

4. Click anywhere outside the file name or hit the enter key.

Why do this? To give a file a more meaningful name.

Find a Lost File

Ideally, you will use the tips and instructions provided in Chapter 3 regarding saving files so that you never "lose" a file. What if you do though? Are you out of luck? Nope. Luckily, Windows XP has a decent search function that can help you find lost files. If you can remember the name, part of the name, or even the date/time you saved the file, you're golden.

1. **Start→Search** (located on the right side of the **Start** menu). The search wizard is now displayed.

2. In the left pane, click on the type of file you want to search for. If you don't know the type of file (music, picture, etc.), click on **All files and folders**.

3. Enter all or part of the filename. Optionally, click on **When was it modified?** and choose a range.

4. Click on **Search**.

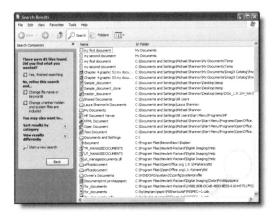

The search wizard searches your computer and displays the results. Notice there is a scroll bar along the bottom of the screen indicating that additional data lies outside the viewable area. Scroll to see everything.

You can click on files and folders in the search window. So if you find the file you're looking for, rename it to something useful (see renaming section) and move it to a more appropriate location.

As you've learned, there are many ways to move and copy files. As long as you have the file displayed in the search wizard, right-click on it and select **Cut**. Then open the folder where you want the file to be via Explorer, right-click in the folder window and select **Paste**.

Delete a File or Folder

1. Navigate to the file you wish to delete.

2. Either select the file and press the **delete** key *o r* drag the file to the **Recycle Bin**. A warning message will appear

asking if you're sure you want to send the file to the **Recycle Bin**.

Performing either of these two actions merely readies the file for deletion – to actually delete the file and recoup the disk space you must empty the **Recycle Bin**.

3. Right-click on the **Recycle Bin** and select **Empty Recycle Bin**. A warning message will appear asking if you're sure you want to delete its contents.

To delete more than one file at a time, use extended selection first (see "select a File or Files" above).

Why do this? You no longer need the file. You need to gain disk space.

Retrieving Deleted Files and Folders

You can retrieve files that are in the **Recycle Bin** before it has been emptied.

1. Double-click on the **Recycle Bin** icon.

2. Select the file(s) you wish to retrieve.

3. Click on **Restore this Item** in the Task Pane. The file will be moved to its original location.

4. You can also cut and paste or click and drag files from the **Recycle Bin** to wherever you'd like.

Why do this? You've decided you want to retain the file after all.

TOP SECRET The files that you place in the Recycle Bin will remain there until one of two things happens:

- You manually empty the Recycle Bin as described above.

- Your hard disk reaches a certain percent full (90% by default) and is emptied automatically.

You can change the percentage point at which the Recycle Bin is auto-emptied or even disable that feature completely by right-clicking on the Recycle Bin and selecting "Properties".

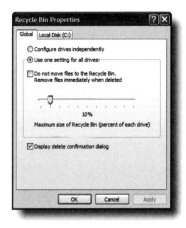

Attach a File to an E-mail

This procedure will vary slightly depending upon your specific e-mail client application or webmail provider.

1. Begin creating and writing an e-mail as normal.

2. Click **Attach Files**.

3. A file requester dialog box is displayed. If not, you may need to click the **Browse** button.

4. Navigate to the file you wish to attach to your e-mail.

5. Click on the file to select it and click the **OK** button or double-click on the file. Note that you can send multiple files with one e-mail by repeating this process. On most webmail services, you will have to click on an **Attach Files** button at this point.

6. Finish the e-mail and click **Send**.

If you are using a POP mail account and either Microsoft Outlook or Mozilla Thunderbird for your mail client, there is another way to attach files which may be easier, particularly when attaching multiple files.

1. Begin creating and writing an e-mail as normal.

2. Open Explorer or use Explore windows to find the file(s) you want to attach.

3. With your mail message next to the window containing the file(s) you want to attach, simply drag the file(s) over

to the e-mail message and release the mouse button.

If the file(s) you are attaching to an e-mail are pictures, there is yet another, perhaps better, way to attach them provided you're using a POP e-mail client, like Outlook or Thunderbird.

1. Navigate to the folder containing the pictures you wish to attach. You can accomplish this by using Explorer, or by selecting **My Pictures** from the **Start** menu.

2. Select the specific picture(s) you want to attach.

3. Click **E-mail this file** from the Task Pane.

Click here to email pictures using a POP email client

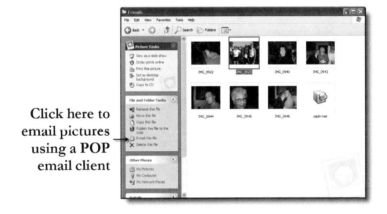

4. This opens a **Send Pictures via E-mail** wizard asking if you'd like to make the pictures smaller before sending.

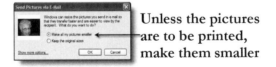

Unless the pictures are to be printed, make them smaller

5. This is an important question. High-resolution digital cameras create pictures that are optimized for printing. The downside of this is that it increases the file size of each picture significantly. Sending huge files via e-mail may exceed the size limit (usually around 5-10 MB) instituted by some ISPs. As a result they may never be delivered. At best, the files will take a very long time for the recipient to download.

So unless you are sending photos that will be printed out at some point, let the wizard reduce (sometimes called "compress") the resolution of your e-mail attachments.

Note that this compression reduces the amount of disk space the pictures use but not their physical size. So if the original picture is 4"x6", the compressed picture will retain that size, but the quality may be less.

6. Once you've answered the resizing question, the wizard goes to work and opens a blank message using your e-mail client with the picture file already attached. Just address, add text, and click send.

Why do this? To send someone a picture, movie, music or other type of file.

TOP SECRET You may be saying to yourself, "Gee, that making the pictures smaller thing seems like a good idea. Too bad I use Yahoo (or other webmail). Guess I am out of luck." Actually, you're not. You can take advantage of Window's built-in compression wizard to reduce picture size and send them through web e-mail services. It just requires a few extra steps.

To do this, follow steps 1-5 above. This will open a new e-mail message, complete with the photos already attached. Even if you haven't configured a POP e-mail client, Microsoft Outlook Express will be set as the default mail client.

Now, just drag the attached file(s) to the Desktop or other location of your choice. Close the incomplete e-mail message (answer "No" to saving) and close Outlook Express.

Open a browser and attach the reduced file onto an e-mail. A little more involved, but the reduction in transfer time is often worth it.

Some graphics programs, such as Paintshop Pro, can also perform image compression.

View and Save a File attached to an E-mail

This gets a bit trickier....

There are two parts to this; saving the file to your hard disk and opening (or viewing) the file.

Generally, you can view or open an attachment without saving it. This is useful as many attachments you receive will be "one shots" – you'll view them once, then toss them. Therefore, this feature saves you a few steps as the attachment will be discarded along with the message if you don't save it.

However, there is a big caveat that goes along with double-clicking a file attachment – it may be harboring something malicious like a virus or a trojan. If you've taken precautions, as outlined in Chapter 10, you're probably safe. It pays to be careful here though.

An e-mail that has a file attached displays a small paper clip icon. Right-clicking on the paper clip usually displays a menu that offers a "Save" or "Save As" command. In this case, after selecting one of the "Save" menu commands, navigate to the location you want to save the file. This will usually be "My Documents" or a sub-directory thereof. Note that you can usually change the file name at this time. So if you know what the file contains, and it is named something meaningless, now is your chance to change it to something better.

Once you've saved the file to your hard disk, navigate to its location and double-click on it. If you have an application that is associated with that particular file type, the application will open and display the file. If this happens, you're golden!

If your PC does not have an application associated with that particular file type, a dialog box will be displayed asking you to select an application that will open that file type. This is not good and could cause some extreme frustration – you have a file and you must see what it contains! In most cases, this means you don't have an application that will work with the file, so you'll need to obtain one. Ask the sender what program created the file as a starting point.

The other aspect of this circumstance is that your e-mail client, or even webmail, may automatically display the file if it is a common file type, such as jpeg or gif. Therefore, explicitly opening an attachment is unnecessary. Check your e-mail client's preference settings or options to see if you can display common file types automatically. Keep in mind that even if the file is displayed automatically, you'll still have to manually save the attachment if you want to keep it. Otherwise, the attachment gets sent to the trash along with the message.

For example, in Thunderbird this option is under the **View** menu as **Display Attachments Inline**.

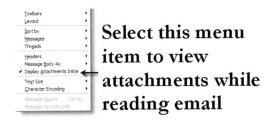

Select this menu item to view attachments while reading email

Switch between Open Applications

Many times, you'll have multiple applications open at the same time. For instance, you may be working on a word processing document while using a web browser to do research. As only one application can be active at a time, you need to switch between them.

There are several ways to switch between open applications:

● Click the task bar button of an application to bring it to the front, making it selected or active.

If the Taskbar button has a number surrounded by parentheses, this indicates that multiple documents are open in that particular application. This is known as "grouping". Clicking the Taskbar button of a grouping displays a menu where you can select specific documents.

- Click anywhere in the application's window you wish to make active – if you can see it.

- Alt + Tab – Hold down the "alt" key with your left thumb, then repeatedly press the "tab" key with your middle finger. This displays a floating box with icons of all running applications. To select one, just press the tab key until the icon is highlighted and release the alt key. To move backwards through the icons, hold down the shift key. This is very handy and permits switching without using the mouse!

Remove an Application

1. **Start → Control Panel → Add or Remove Programs**.

2. Select the application you want to remove.

3. Click the **Remove** button. The hamsters inside of Windows will go to work and in a few minutes (it will just seem like hours), present you with a dialog box informing you that the application has been removed.

Click on item to remove, then click the "Change/Remove" button

4. **Why do this?** You may wish to remove an application you don't use to free up disk space or just to decrease clutter.

Importing Pictures from a Digital Camera

With previous versions of Windows, getting pictures from a digital camera into a PC was non-intuitive at best. It required the user to load additional software supplied with the specific camera. Obviously not an insurmountable problem, but if you wanted to transfer photos to a friend's PC while on vacation, you best hope you brought that CD of software....

Windows XP's handling of this task is much, much better. Essentially, Windows XP has all the software needed to transfer photos from the camera to the PC already built in – if your digital camera is WIA (Windows Image Acquisition) compliant. Most digital cameras manufactured since 2000 are WIA-compliant.[*]

Here's how it works:

1. Plug the USB cable included with your camera into the camera itself.

2. Plug the other end of the USB cable into a USB port on your PC.

3. A "Scanner and Camera" wizard appears and offers to hold your hand through the importation process.

---

[*] If, by chance, you have a camera that is not WIA-compliant, you'll have to install the software that was included with the camera. Check the manufacturer's website first to ensure you have the latest version.

Click the
"Advanced
users only"
hyperlink to
display
pictures in
Explorer

At this point you can click **Next** and follow the instructions on each screen of the wizard. It is extremely simple to use. You may wish however, to flaunt your new found file wrangling skills and instead, click on the **Advanced Users Only** hyperlink located in the middle of the previous screen.

This dangerous sounding link actually presents you with a view of the photos on your camera that you should now be very familiar with – the Folders view.

Select "Thumbnails" from
the "View" menu to
display small versions of
your pictures

Now, when first displayed the files may appear as icons, but a trivial change of the **View** menu to **Thumbnails** will show you small representations of your photos.

To transfer these photos to your hard disk, use any standard file manipulation technique you're comfortable with. Either cut and paste selected photos or drag and drop to the location of your choice. You can also select files and use the "Copy this file" link located on the Task Pane.

Clicking the "**For Advanced Users Only**" link presents the camera as if it were just another attached storage device – which is exactly what it is.

As a slight aside, if you purchase one of the many available portable MP3 players, such as an Apple iPod, you'll find that it works exactly the same way – plug it in to the PC and it appears as a removable storage device, just drag and drop files of your choice.

View your Pictures with an Onscreen Slide Show

You can easily create a self-advancing, full-screen slide show of the pictures contained on your PC.

1. Select **My Pictures** from the **Start** menu. You can also use any folder that contains pictures.

2. Click the **View as slide show** link under **Picture Tasks** on the Task Pane. The display turns black and the entire screen is filled with your personal photos. Every five seconds the picture changes to the next one in the folder.

3. If you move the mouse, a floating palette of movie controls appears in the upper right of the screen allowing you play, pause, rewind, advance or stop the slide show.

4. Pressing the escape key halts the slide show.

TOP SECRET The above procedure works for any folder that contains pictures. You may notice however, that photo-related tasks only appear on the Task Pane of "My Pictures". This is because the "My Pictures" folder has the "Photo Album" or "Pictures" theme applied. You can manually apply these themes to any folder you wish by right-clicking the folder, selecting "Properties", and then clicking on the "Customize" tab.

In addition to the above method, you can also display a slide show whenever your computer is idle for a period of time you select. Here's how:

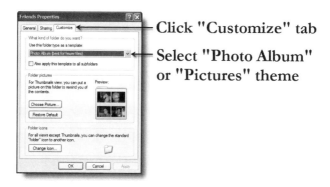

Click "Customize" tab

Select "Photo Album" or "Pictures" theme

1. Right-click the **Desktop** and select **Properties**. Then click the **Screen Saver** tab.

2. Select **My Pictures Slide Show** from the drop-down box. If you want to change the interval between pictures or use a folder other than **My Pictures**, click the **Settings** button.

251

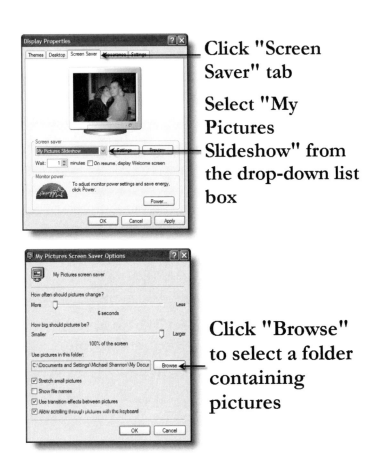

Click "Screen Saver" tab

Select "My Pictures Slideshow" from the drop-down list box

Click "Browse" to select a folder containing pictures

Burning Files to a CD

Like importing pictures from a digital camera, saving files onto a CD used to be quite an ordeal. Now, it's only a *slight* ordeal.

Honestly, it is fairly easy to do once you understand that even though CDs (and DVDs) appear as standard Windows storage media, they don't quite act like it in at least one regard – that being the way files are saved.

With most storage media, such as hard disks, floppies, Zip disks and flash drives, you simply cut and paste or drag and drop files seamlessly between disks. CDs require an extra step. That step is what is referred to as "burning". So the general idea is, you select files that you want to copy to a CD, you move them to a "staging area", then you burn them onto the CD.

This procedure applies to copying data files to a CD that will be used on a PC. If you want to create a custom music CD to play in a standard audio CD player, see the next two sections.

To burn files to a CD:

1. Confirm that you have a CD-R or CD-RW drive. These drives allow you to create CDs. A CD-ROM drive can only read disks. Also, make sure you have a blank CD compatible with your particular drive.

2. Insert the blank disk into the drive. A dialog box appears asking if you'd like to **Open writable CD folder**.

3. Click **OK** and an Explorer window appears showing the contents of the CD, which is blank.

4. Now, you must place the files that you want to copy onto the CD into the Explorer window. You can use any method you wish to navigate to the files you want to add to the CD. Then use **Copy** and **Paste**, drag and drop, or right-click on the file(s) and select **Send to→CD Drive**.

5. When you have placed all the files you want into the CD drive window, click on the **Write these files to CD** hyperlink located in the Task Pane. Note that the files have a down arrow attached indicating that they have not yet been burned to the CD. This comes in handy later on when you want to add files (this is only possible if you have a re-writable CD drive) to this CD – you can easily tell which files are not yet burned.

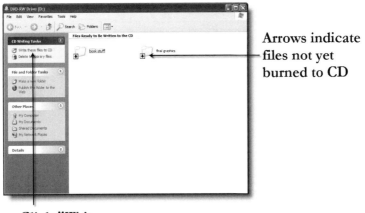

Arrows indicate files not yet burned to CD

Click "Write these files to CD" hyperlink to burn files to CD

6. The CD Writing wizard opens and asks you to name the new CD. Pick anything you want, though you won't be able to change it later.

7. The last screen of the wizard asks if you'd like to make another copy of the CD you've just burned. This comes in handy when making your friends illegal copies of all the

MP3 files you have.

TOP SECRET Standard re-writable CDs hold either 650 or 700MB of data. To make sure that the files you are about to copy onto the CD will fit, select all of them in the CD window before writing (ctrl-A selects everything in a window) and look at the "Details" box located in the Task Pane to analyze the cumulative size.

Playing and Copying Music with your PC

Using a PC to copy, manipulate, and share music has become "the next big thing" over the last few years. You have several options regarding this topic:

- **Play music CDs using your PC** – You can use your PC as you would any standard CD player.

- **Copy music CDs onto your computer** – This process takes songs from music CDs and transforms them into digital music files. This process is known as "ripping", such as "I have a bunch of CDs I need to rip". This allows you to listen to your songs in the order you desire and create custom playlists containing hours of music. Once your CDs are copied onto your hard disk, you can easily transfer them to a portable digital music player, such as an Apple iPod or other MP3 player. You can also trade music with other people to greatly enlarge your collection for free, though technically this violates copyright laws and is illegal. You can even make a custom playlist and burn songs onto a CD (if you have a CD burner) that will play in any standard audio player!

- **Purchase music online** – Several online stores sell music in digital format. Some even allow you to purchase individual songs, such as Apple's iTunes store. Songs are $.99 each.

There are several applications that can perform the above tasks. Windows Media Player (WMP) is included with Windows. Depending on your particular PC, you may have other music players installed as well. Many PCs now ship with iTunes from Apple already installed. Both of these applications should fulfill all of your music needs. In fact, with version 10 of Windows Media Player, Microsoft seems to have virtually copied iTunes.

My personal preference is iTunes, due to its straight-forward interface, and the fact that WMP constantly tries to connect to the Internet to transfer who knows what back to Microsoft.

Regardless of which application you have installed, they both work similarly and you should have no trouble transferring instructions for one program to the other.

Play a Music CD

1. Insert a music CD into the CD drive.

2. The drive spins and in a moment a dialog box appears asking you what you'd like to do with the CD.

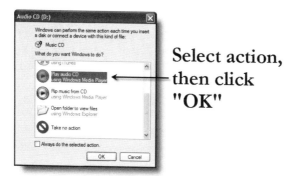

Select action, then click "OK"

Note that in this case, the PC I am using came pre-configured with both WMP and iTunes so the dialog box is listing options pertaining to both programs. Your specific options will vary depending upon the applications installed on your PC. Also, **Import songs** and **Rip music from CD** are equivalent. iTunes uses the term **Import** in place of **Rip**. Click **Play audio CD** then click the **OK** button. If you click the **Always do the selected action** checkbox, Windows will not display this dialog box next time you insert a music CD and instead, just carry on with the task. If you check this box and then decide at some other point that you want to do something else, such as rip music tracks, you can still do that from within the application.

3. The application opens and begins to play the songs on the CD.

4. You can change the order songs play, enable visualizations – abstract screen art – and many other options by using the menus and tool bars in the application.

Ripping (Importing) Songs onto a PC

The ripping process takes standard audio CDs and copies their music tracks onto a PC. At the same time, it transforms them into a digital music file format called MP3. However, you can change this format in the application's preferences.

Try it:

1. Insert a music CD into the CD drive.

2. The drive spins and in a moment a dialog box appears asking you what you'd like to do with the CD. In this case, you'll select either **Import songs** or **Rip music from CD,** depending upon which program you want to use or have available to you.

3. The application opens and begins copying/transforming the music tracks. If your PC is connected by a broadband Internet connection, WMP or iTunes will automatically attempt to download album, artist, and track information. This information is then added to your music library automatically and makes it possible to create playlists based on artist, album, or genre.

4. The location where ripped music is stored is by default **My Music,** though you can change this and many other properties in both programs. Click the two checkboxes for **Rip CD when inserted** and **Eject CD when ripping is complete**. Then take all your CDs and shuffle them into the drive as you watch TV. In a few hours, you'll have your whole music collection transferred onto your PC!

TOP SECRET Along with the storage location of digital music and other properties, one very important option to choose before you begin ripping music is what digital music format to use.

Traditionally, MP3 was by far the dominant format. With the advent of online music stores and copyright infringement issues, several other formats are available and popular such as WMA and AAC.

So which should you use? It depends on where you plan to acquire your digital music from and what you intend on doing with it once you have it.

AAC and WMA provide slightly better sound quality than MP3, and if you purchase music online, it will most likely be in AAC or WMA format. The downside is that not all portable digital music players support these two formats, while almost all support MP3.

If you don't have or don't plan on buying a portable music player, then AAC or WMA are probably what you want. Otherwise, I'd suggest MP3 as they'll play on virtually everything.

All of these file formats have options, such as "bit rate", that allow you to produce smaller files, thus allowing you to store more tracks in a finite space. However, as music files are compressed they lose some fidelity, so larger files will sound better. It is a trade-off between storage space and high-quality sound. MP3's are usually encoded at 128 kbps.

This drop-down list box in iTunes determines what file format is used when ripping music from CDs

Burning Audio Music CDs

Once you've acquired a collection of digital music files, either through ripping your own CDs or buying and trading music files, you may want to transform them back to standard audio files and burn them to a CD so they can be played on any standard audio CD player, such as the one in your car.

Several applications offer this capability, including WMP and iTunes. Simply burning digital music files onto a CD will not work, as standard audio CD players cannot play these files.[*]

With either WMP or iTunes the process is essentially the same.

1. Create a custom playlist that contains the music tracks you wish to burn onto a CD. A playlist is nothing more than a list of songs. Select **New Playlist** and drag selected tracks from the main music library onto the playlist you've just created.

---

[*] There are a few stand-alone CD players that do offer this capability, but they are rare.

2. Once you've compiled your playlist and saved it, verify that the settings for burning are set properly to make an audio CD.

3. Burn the CD. In iTunes, click the **Burn Disc** button. In Windows Media Player, click the **Start Burn** icon.

Right-click "My Playlists" and select "New".
Next, drag songs from the library to the new
playlist area on the right

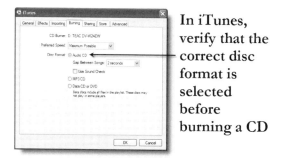

In iTunes,
verify that the
correct disc
format is
selected
before
burning a CD

Chapter 12

Just the FAQs...

Once you get connected to the Internet and start doing a bit of poking around, you're likely to come across documents on various topics with the letters "FAQ" in the title. FAQ is an acronym for "Frequently Asked Questions", though a better phrase might be "Frequently Answered Questions". FAQ is pronounced much like the word "fax" or "facts".

FAQs are documents that list and answer the most common questions on a particular topic. Usually written by folks that are tired of answering the same questions over and over, FAQs exist for virtually any topic you can think of, from gardening to computers to specific breeds of dogs.

Shown below are the results of a web search for the words "pug" and "faq":

Enter topic plus the word "faq"

Search results

FAQs are a great way to research any topic and should be your starting point. Simply type the topic of choice into your favorite search engine (or the FireFox search bar), along with

263

the word "faq".

When searching the Internet for information, keep in mind the following tips:

- Using capital letters will only find words that are capitalized exactly how you entered them. Using lower-case letters will also find words that are capitalized.

- Place multiple terms inside quotes to find the exact phrase. Terms separated by spaces will find any web pages that contain those terms anywhere on the page. For example, "homebrew beer yeast" will find any web pages that contain that exact phrase. Leaving off the quotes will find any web page that has those three words anywhere on the page.

In this chapter, I've listed and answered many FAQs of new computer users. If you have a question that hasn't been addressed previously in the book, chances are good the answer is here. If your question isn't answered here, e-mail it to me at computersecrets@smartguypress.com and I may include it in the next printing.

Q: Why does everything I type display in all capital letters?

A: You've inadvertently pressed the caps lock key. Most keyboards have a caps lock light to indicate this. Press the caps lock key again to turn it off.

Q: When I press the number keys on the keypad next to the alpha keys nothing happens. Why is this?

A: You need to turn num lock on. Pres the num lock key once.

Q: The computer keeps beeping at me! Why is it doing this?

A: You've asked it to do something that it cannot do. Perhaps you're trying to type in a window that is not selected or you've repeatedly pressed a key or clicked the mouse when the PC is not ready for such input.

TOP SECRET Computers can't sense frustration. Pressing keys multiple times or clicking a close box again and again does nothing but cause the computer to function more slowly. Users sometimes do these things because they feel that the PC is not responding fast enough. So, they repeat their last action over and over, hoping the PC will eventually "get it" and do what they want. If you click a button, select a menu command, or press a key and nothing seems to be happening, wait ten seconds and repeat the action. If that still doesn't work, the PC is busy with a task and you must wait until it completes before continuing.

Q: I am working in a word processing application and there are all kinds of weird symbols appearing after my sentences and dots between words. Why?

A: You inadvertently turned on "show non-printing characters". Most word processors have an option to show the non-printing characters the program uses for formatting text. The dots between the words indicates spaces and the symbol at the end of each paragraph (looks kind of like a reversed "P") indicates its end. This can be useful when proofing a document. Depending on the word processor, turning this function on/off may be done through an options/preferences menu or a toolbar icon. OpenOffice uses a toolbar icon that looks like the paragraph symbol to toggle this function. Try searching for "non-printing characters" in help. As indicated by the term "non-printing", even though these characters show up on screen, they'll be absent if you print the document.

¶

**Paragraph
Symbol**

Q: I made one word bold and now everything after it is bold also. How do I fix it?

A: Bold, *italic*, and <u>underline</u> are toggles. Clicking bold turns it on for everything after that point until you toggle it off. To correct your problem, select the text you don't want to be bold. (hold down left mouse button and drag) Be sure and select everything, which may include a hidden character after the sentence. (See question above.) Then click on the bold toolbar icon.

Q: Something happened and now the Taskbar (program bar along the bottom of the screen) is missing. How do I get it back?

A: This is a very common problem and one that throws off a lot of new users. The Taskbar is movable and resizable. If it's missing completely, you inadvertently resized it to almost nothing. To get it back, move the arrow cursor close to the bottom of the screen. Now, very slowly continue to move the cursor down. Just before you get to the very bottom of the screen, the cursor will change from the default arrow cursor to a very thin arrow that points upward. When this happens, stop moving the cursor, hold down the left mouse button, and slowly move the mouse straight up. The Taskbar will reappear.

You can prevent this from ever happening in the first place by locking the Taskbar. Right-click on a blank area of the Taskbar and select "Lock the Taskbar". Now the Taskbar will be immune from any attempt to move or resize it. If you decide you do want to move or resize the Taskbar, simply reselect the "Lock the Taskbar" menu item so that the check mark disappears.

Q: The Taskbar that was along the bottom of my screen is now on the side/top of my screen? How do I get it back to the bottom.

A: Simply hold down the left mouse button on any empty area of the Taskbar and drag it to wherever you'd like it to be.

Q: Can I get something back that I threw into the Recycle Bin?

A: Depends. The Recycle Bin acts just like any other folder until you right-click on it and select "Empty Recycle Bin". So, if you've only moved something to the Recycle Bin, you can open it (either by double-clicking or through Explorer) and take out your file. However, if you have already emptied the Recycle Bin, the file is gone forever.

Q: How do I install new software?

A: First, verify that the software you plan on installing is designed for Windows XP (or whatever OS you're using). Then, make sure you are logged on with an account that has system administrator privileges. Next, follow the instructions provided with the software *to the letter*. This occasionally varies, but usually consists of putting a CD in the drive and clicking through an install wizard that asks you various questions.

Q: How do I install new hardware?

A: There are many different "peripherals" - PC gadgets such as scanners, webcams, game joysticks, upgraded sound and video cards, wireless networking routers and cards. As your experience grows you might want to add some of these to your system.

Generally, I am against upgrading core system components such as video and sound cards, CPUs, and hard drives. This is because it often makes more sense, both financially and in terms of practicality and troubleshooting, to simply purchase a new, state-of-the-art PC every four or five years. This way, you get the latest components and operating system software and avoid the hassle of trying to get everything to work together.

Adding printers, webcams, joysticks and scanners is certainly acceptable and easy to do. This is particularly true if the gadget connects to the PC via USB.

Regardless of the hardware you're installing, the number one rule is to follow the manufacturer's instructions to the letter. They've created and developed the product, they should know exactly how to install it and make it work.

The basic installation ritual usually consists of installing software included with the hardware, known as a "driver" and then physically connecting the hardware. If the hardware is connected via USB, you can plug it right in. No need to even turn off the PC. This is known as being "hot swappable". Components that plug into other ports or slots may need to be connected while the PC is turned

268

off. Again, follow the manufacturer's instructions.

Q: Sometimes I point at an icon and the tooltip text says it is a "shortcut". What is a shortcut?

A: Shortcuts are pointers to something else. They are of course files, but these files only hold the location information of other files. They exist to aid in organization.

For example, let's assume you use the FireFox browser to surf web pages. FireFox, by default, is installed in "c:\program files\mozilla firefox". This makes sense as FireFox is a program, and most programs are stored in the "program files" folder.

Or course, you need an easy way to start FireFox. You could open Explorer, navigate to "c:\program files\mozilla firefox", and double-click the FireFox icon, but that is time-consuming. A faster, easier way to start FireFox would be to have an icon on your Desktop, Quicklaunch bar, Start menu, or even all three of these areas!

This can easily be accomplished with shortcuts. Create shortcuts to any file by right-clicking and selecting "Create Shortcut". The shortcut is created in the same folder. You can move, copy, and rename the shortcut just like any other file. Shortcuts are differentiated from other files by a small black arrow in the lower left corner of the icon. This arrow does not display if the shortcut is in the Start menu or Quicklaunch bar.

To place a shortcut on the Desktop, Start menu, or Quicklaunch bar, just drag it wherever you want it.

Q: I've seen confusing text in several places, particularly when installing software, such as "c:\my name\my documents\my file". What does all of that mean?

A: That is simply a way of indicating a file location or technically, a "full-path name" or "fully-qualified path". You typically see it during software installs as the install wizard is asking you to select a location to install the software.

It's easy to decipher this "code":

The starting letter and colon, in the above example "c:" indicates the drive the file is stored on. By default, "c:" is the first internal hard disk. Other disks, whether additional hard disks, CD drives, DVD drives or others, are assigned sequential alphabetic letters; such as "d:", "e:", "f" and so on. Floppy drives, which your system may or may not have, are always "a:".

The backslash ("\") indicates a division and is placed between the drive and folder, between folder and folder, and between folder and file.

The last name in the full path is a file name. All names between the drive and the file name are folders.

For example, let's decipher "c:\documents and settings\Michael Shannon\my documents\typing practice\typing sentence.txt".

"c:" is the internal hard disk.

"\documents and settings\Michael Shannon\my documents\typing practice\" are four folders or directories.

"typing practice.txt" is the file name.

The full path we just deciphered looks like this when viewed in Explorer:

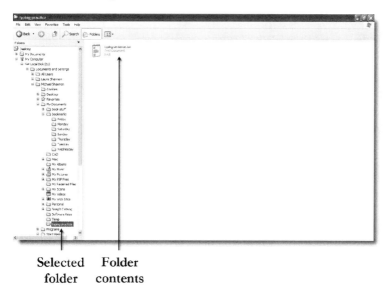

Selected **Folder**
folder **contents**

Q: How do I know what version of Windows I have?

A: You would think that finding the Windows' version would be simple and obvious – yet ,it isn't. At least it wasn't to me.

The simplest way is: **Start→run** and enter "winver". This runs a program, called not surprisingly, "winver", which displays a Windows "About" box.

271

 **Windows version information**

As you can see in the above graphic, my system is running Windows XP Service Pack 2.

An alternate way is: **Start→My Computer** and click on "System Information".

Q: How do I know what version of a particular application I have?

A: While the program is open, select **Help→About.** This displays version information.

Q: What is DOS?

A: Remember in Chapter 1 when I went over older computer systems, GUIs, and command line interfaces? Well, DOS is the command line interface of Windows. Technically, DOS stands for "Disk Operating System". In past releases of Windows, DOS was a more integral part of the operating system. With the release of XP, DOS is more a legacy portion of the OS that is rarely needed. Note I said "rarely"...

Related to DOS, is the "Run..." menu selection located in the Start menu. Selecting "Run..." displays a dialog box. This box requires the name of a program or a DOS command for input. You can also open the DOS command line interface itself by entering "cmd" in the "Run..." box. Type "exit" to close the DOS interface. I knew you'd try it....

DOS
Commands

Enter
commands
here

Again, normally you're not going to need to use either DOS or the "Run..." command.

Q: Why are some programs on my Start menu highlighted with a pink/orange color?

A: I have to admit, this one initially threw me as well. The highlighted items are newly installed. Windows XP highlights these items and pops up a little box saying "Newly installed programs" the first time you click on "Start" after programs are installed.

If this annoys you, it can be turned off. Right-click on **Start**, select **Properties**, click on **Customize**, then click the **Advanced** tab. Uncheck the **Highlight newly installed programs** check box.

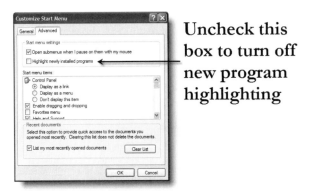

Uncheck this box to turn off new program highlighting

Q: Why are there two "X" close boxes in the upper right corner when I am using certain applications?

A: The top "X" close button that is red (if you haven't manually altered the color scheme) is the close button for the application. Clicking on it will either:

● Close the application and all open documents, if the documents have been saved.

● Pop up a dialog box asking if you want to save any unsaved changes to your open documents. Upon your response, it will close the application and documents.

The "X" close button located below the red "X" is the document close button. Clicking this "X" will either:

● Close the current active document if it is already saved, and leave the application open.

● Pop up a dialog box asking if you want to save any

changes to the active document. It will then close just the document, leaving the application open.

This is useful, for example, if you've just finished writing a letter and wish to close it but would like to leave the application open in order to create a new letter.

Note that the lower "X" close button is exactly the same as selecting "Close" from the file menu.

Q: When trying to rename a file, the computer beeps and tells me that a file with that file name already exists. However, I see other files with the same names. What's the deal?

A: The rule is simple regarding files with the exact same name – they can't be located in the same folder. So, you can have as many copies of "letter to mom" as you want, as long as they are in different folders. Now you may be thinking "No way, I am looking at a folder right now and I see two files with the exact same name". You just *think* you see two files with the *exact* same name.... If you have file extensions turned off, two or more files may appear to have the exact same names. The difference is that they have different extensions. So, "letter to mom.doc" and "letter to mom.txt" may appear to be the same, but are actually different. Hover the mouse over each file to display a tooltip that identifies the file type.

Q: How come when I copy and paste text it doesn't always appear exactly as it did when it was copied?

A: When pasting text between different applications, text formatting, that is bold, italic, underline, color, etc., may not be interpreted the same, so you just get plain text.

However, if you're copying and pasting between Microsoft programs, such as Office or Internet Explorer, you should be fine. If you do it between other applications, it will be hit or miss.

Q: There is a file on my Desktop that looks like a torn piece of paper. I didn't put it there. What is it?

A: Actually, you or someone else that uses your PC did put it there. It was probably put there inadvertently. The "scrap" as it is called, is created when text is selected (highlighted) and then dragged from an application onto the Desktop. Windows automatically transforms this text into a scrap file, the contents of which is the selected text. The file name reflects the program that created the file, and if you hover the mouse over the scrap icon for a few seconds, the first few words of the file will be displayed. Double-clicking on the scrap opens the file in the application that created it.

Q: In my high-school typing class I was taught to put one space between words and two spaces between sentences. My friend says this isn't true with computers. Who is right?

A: Your friend is correct. Typewriters used fixed-pitch fonts. That is, every character, whether an "i" or a "w", uses exactly the same amount of space. Modern PCs use proportional fonts where each character uses only the

276

space it needs. Hence, use one space between words and only one space between sentences. Really.

Here's an example:

```
This is a fixed-pitch font commonly
used on typewriters, called Courier.
Notice how all the letters line up
exactly with the letters on the line
above. This is why two spaces are
required between sentences.
```

This is a proportional font. Each character in the font uses only the space it requires. Notice that the "i" in this font is right up tight against the letters to either side of it. Also notice that unlike the Courier text above, these characters do not line up exactly in columns.

Q: Why do some folders offer a "Filmstrip" option on the view menu while others don't?

A: One of the design goals of Windows XP was to make it "multi-media savvy". So, several features were added to ease dealing with pictures, digital cameras, and scanners. The "Filmstrip" view option is one of these new features that offers several useful shortcuts when dealing with image files. This is especially true when working with a digital camera.

The options offered in the View menu, as well as the options offered on the Task Pane, are controlled by the folder "template". This template is a predefined set of options that you can assign to any folder. Select "Customize This Folder" from the "View" menu.

Feel free to change options just to see what will happen. You can always return everything to its original condition by clicking the "Restore Default" button.

Select "Photo Album" or "Pictures" from the drop-down list box to enable "Filmstrip" view

TOP SECRET If you hold down the shift key while selecting "Thumbnails" from the "View" menu, or while double-clicking a folder using the "Photo Album" or "Pictures" template, the file names will disappear giving you more space in the window. To get them back, just repeat the process holding down the shift key again.

Q: How do I insert a symbol, such as a copyright or trademark, into a text document?

A: Symbols, sometimes called "special characters" can be inserted in a few different ways.

Many applications that format text offer a "Special Character" command usually located on the "Insert" menu if one exists. Selecting this menu command displays a dialog box where you can view all the characters available for each installed font. To use a character, select it, then click the "OK" button to insert it at the current cursor location.

Additionally, Windows offers a built-in application, called "Character Map", just for this purpose. You can access Character Map through **Start** → **All Programs** → **Accessories** → **System Tools** → **Character Map**.

Select font

Click on character

Click "Select", then "Copy", then paste into your document

To use Character Map, select a font from the drop-down box located near the top. Then select a character by clicking on it. Next, click the "Select" button. This copies the character to the Windows clipboard. To use it, simply select "paste" anywhere you can enter text.

In addition to common symbols like ™ and ©, you'll also find small graphics known as "wingdings", "webdings", or "dingbats". Check for fonts using these names and you'll have access to hundreds of interesting graphics you can use and resize just like letters. Here are a few examples:

Q: What's a "backup" and do I need to make them?

A: Backups are just additional copies of important files. If accidentally deleting a file would cause you grief, you may want to make a backup. Ideally, you'll want to save the backup file to a different storage device, thus reducing your risk should your hard disk fail.

A CD or DVD writable drive is perfect for backups, though the new, inexpensive "flash" drives are even more convenient. Flash drives are small, portable devices that plug into the USB port and appear to Windows as a removable drive.

TOP SECRET **If you purchase a portable MP3 player, such as an Apple iPod, you can use it to store backups of important files. Aside from the ability to play music files, Windows XP sees these devices as just another type of removable storage. Plug the player into your PC and drag whatever files you'd like over to the player – instant backup! I use my Sandisk MP3 player to back up my important files every day.**

Q: Is there any way to put digital pictures on a CD or DVD so that they can be shown on a TV using a stand alone DVD player?

A: Yes, but you will need a CD or DVD writable drive, often called a "burner", and additional software. Several companies make commercial products that can produce slide shows of digital photos that play on standard living room DVD players. Two popular products for this are Sonic MyDVD Studio and Nero Photo Show.

Q: Whenever I send an e-mail, the program displays a dialog box asking whether I want to use "plaintext" or "HTML". Which do I want to use?

A: HTML stands for "Hypertext Markup Language" and is the primary language used to format web pages. Plaintext is just ordinary text, often called "ASCII" text.

Using HTML for e-mail messages offers two advantages over plaintext:

1. You can send website addresses, known as "URLs", and the recipient can simply click on the address to open the site in a browser. The address will show up in the e-mail as a underlined hyperlink.

2. Text formatting, such as **bold**, *italic*, and underlined is displayed.

Essentially, HTML allows your messages to look pretty. So why wouldn't you always want to use HTML for e-mail? Not everyone uses the same e-mail client, or even the same type of computer system. Some e-mail clients don't support HTML and most that do allow the user to disable this function. In these cases, HTML formatted e-mails display the embedded HTML codes. At best, this makes the message difficult to read. At worst, it can obscure it completely.

The best bet is to use plaintext. Your messages might not look as "pretty", but this ensures that the recipient receives your message the same way as you sent it. Another option with some e-mail clients, notably Thunderbird, is to send the message as both plaintext and HTML.

Q: Is there any way to save an image I saw on a web page?

A: Yes, but keep in mind that by doing so you may be violating someone's copyright to that image. If you're saving it for strictly personal usage, I'd say you're in the clear.

Just right-click on the image itself while viewing the page in your browser and select **Save Image As**. A save dialog box will appear. Navigate to the location you wish to save the image, give it a meaningful name, and click **Save**.

Q: Why do some website addresses (URLs) have .org or .tv at the end instead of .com?

A: The last few letters of the URL after the period (called "dot"), are known as the "domain extension". While .com is the most common, several others exist, such as: .net, . info, .biz and .org. In addition, there are many different country extensions such as .co.uk for Britain and .de for Germany.

Chapter 13

Where to go from Here

The path to computer expertise is a never ending one. Consider this book as several rungs on the learning ladder. Even though you've already learned a considerable amount, there is always more to absorb, new applications to conquer, hardware upgrades to install.

Learn to Type

I am constantly amazed by the number of people, including computer professionals who are on the keyboard all day, who cannot type. I am talking about touch-typing here. Occasionally I am surprised by how fast someone can "hunt and peck", but this speed will never approach that of even an average touch-typist. Taking the time to learn to touch-type may seem unworthy, but the contrary is true. Learning to type will absolutely be one of the best things you can do if you're serious about learning and using computers. And before you automatically dismiss learning to type as requiring too much time or effort, think again. It can take a surprisingly short time to learn touch-typing. I learned in less than two weeks, practicing about 20 minutes per day. Today I can easily type 70 words per minute. So maybe now you're at least considering learning, but the deal breaker is signing up for a class. Not to worry! The best, most efficient, and easiest way to learn to touch-type is by using the PC itself.

Several brands of typing tutor software are available. Essentially this software offers progressive on-screen exercises to train your fingers. In addition, most also include speed and accuracy drills with feedback and statistics. Many of these programs automatically adjust the exercises they offer based on your specific weaknesses. So if you're having some trouble using the pinkie fingers on both hands, the exercises will adjust and give you more practice on that.

I'd love to give a specific recommendation for a typing tutor application, but it has been years since I learned and the program I used is long off the market. I have done considerable research on the topic though, and many people highly recommend Garfield's Typing Pal Deluxe. For less than $20, this is all you need to successfully learn touch-typing. How can you resist the opportunity to "Play with Garfield, Odie, and their friends as you develop essential keyboarding skills?" You can download a free demo of this product from http://garfield.typingpal.com/. You can purchase it from amazon.com or a local software store.

Changing Things to your Liking

For most people, personal computers are tools – implements used for specific tasks. With some tools – for example a hammer – the method of usage is obvious; you grab it and pound things. It's very simple to operate and there really are no other options.

PCs are a bit more complicated. However, one of the things that can reduce this complication (or increase it, depending on your point of view) is to alter the tool to your preferences.

Once you've become comfortable with PC basics – navigating around Windows, starting and using applications, and opening and saving files, you may want to change some of the ways that Windows works or appears.

When you're a total novice, changing these properties doesn't make much sense. For one thing, a novice won't really have a thorough understanding of what changing properties will really accomplish and hasn't yet formed any ideas or habits about how he or she works. Therefore, I really recommend waiting until you know the basics before changing any of Window's often bewildering number of options and properties.

Make no mistake though, once you decide to start changing things you can really chew up some serious time. With XP, Microsoft has enabled users to change virtually every aspect of the way Windows works and appears.

Changing these parameters is really all about customizing your PC to how you work and how you want things to appear. There is no right or wrong, only personal preference.

Whenever I get a new PC, there are several changes I automatically make based on my years of experience. Within a very short time you'll know exactly how you like things.

Here are just a few of the things you might wish to change:

- **Mouse settings** – Speed, double-click sensitivity, hide cursor while typing.

- **Keyboard** – Cursor blink rate, delay before key repeats.

- **Windows appearance** – Background picture or pattern (often called Desktop wallpaper), themes (how windows appear and what color).

- **Screen saver** – What screen saver appears after the PC has been inactive for a set period of time.

- **Start menu** – You can change not only the look of the Start menu, but also rearrange programs in any order you like by grabbing and dragging. This works for the Quick Launch area also.

- **Sounds** – You can select "sound themes", which automatically assign sounds to specific Window's events, such as error beeps or emptying the Recycle Bin.

- **E-mail Filters** – These filters can automatically delete mail based on rules you configure.

Recommendations and more Secrets

While you're free to configure settings to your desires, you may be interested in what an experienced user finds most helpful. The following are tips, tricks, and recommendations that you may at least want to consider when adjusting things within Windows.

- Previous versions of Windows had a very useful feature, especially for newbies, called "My Recent Documents". This feature still exists within XP, but is hidden by default. This is a menu command located on the Start menu. Hovering the mouse over "My Recent Documents" displays a list of the fifteen documents you've most recently opened. This can be a godsend for newbies not familiar with the Windows file structure. It's also very useful as an experienced user, as you don't have to burrow through various folders to open a document. To turn on the "My Recent Documents" menu:

1. Right-click **Start**.

2. Select **Properties**.

3. Click the **Start menu** tab.

4. Click the **Customize** button.

5. Click the **Advanced** tab.

6. Click the "**List my most recently opened documents**" checkbox and then the "**OK**" button.

7. Click **Start** to view the results.

Check this box to display a list of recently opened documents on your Start menu

"Hey, where did all my documents go!" You may run into a situation where you sit down to use your PC, mouse over to Start → My Recent Documents only to find nothing there or documents that you've never seen before. If this happens, check the name that appears on the top of the Start menu. Chances are you're logged on as someone else. Each unique Windows XP account has a separate My Documents area and a separate My Recent Documents area. To fix this, log off and then log back on as yourself.

Chapter 14

Glossary

Active – Usually refers to a window ready for use; also called "selected". Only one window can be active at a time.

Adware – Small applications designed to display advertising. Usually installed without the user's knowledge.

All-In-One Device – An external device containing a scanner, copier, printer and optionally, a fax machine. Highly recommended.

Applet – A small application designed to do one specific task, such as deliver weather forecasts or stock quotes.

Application – Also called "program". Software designed and used for a particular task. Not associated with system software or the "operating system".

Arrow – A type of cursor. Its movement is connected to the mouse and is used to point to and click on objects. See also "cursor".

ASCII – Pronounced "askey"; an acronym for *American Standard Code for Information Interchange*. This is an agreed upon standard for representing common alphanumeric text with numerical equivalents. This allows different types of computers and software to exchange information.

Backspace (key) – Pressing the backspace key moves the text cursor one space to the left, deleting the character currently there.

Backup – A second copy of a data file used in case the original is damaged.

BIOS – An acronym for *Basic Input Output System*. BIOS is software permanently stored on a computer chip in a PC. It controls hardware and starts the boot process by loading system software.

Boot – Starting the computer by loading the system software.

Bounce – To return e-mail for one or more reasons. Usually due to an incorrect or invalid address. The bounced e-mail is returned to you with a terse explanation of what went wrong.

Browser – An application used primarily for viewing web pages. Other applications exist however, such as image browsers, used to view graphics stored on your PC.

Bug – An error in software. Requires recoding the application.

Cache – A space used for temporary storage of data.

CPU – *Central Processing Unit*. The main computing chip used in computers. The most common CPUs are made by Intel and AMD.

Circuit Board – A thin, usually fiberglass, board on which the CPU and other chips are mounted. The main board is called the mother board.

Clip Board – A virtual (meaning you can't see it) space where information can be copied to and from.

Close Button – The "X" that appears in the upper right

corner of all windows. Clicking this button closes the window.

Control Key – Usually abbreviated as "ctrl", these keys are located on both sides of the space bar. Used in conjunction with other keys for shortcuts.

Control Panel – A location within Windows XP that contains applications which hold settings for various parameters such as mouse, printer, and display properties. Accessed through the "Start" menu.

Cookie – A small file stored on a PC containing information used by a specific website. For example, Amazon stores a cookie that contains personal information on your PC. When you log on the Amazon, the site reads this cookie and welcomes you by your actual name.

Crash – Used to describe an error that causes a program to freeze or stop working. Some crashes will require rebooting the computer.

Cursor – Typically refers to the blinking line which indicates where text will be entered. Also refers to the pointer or arrow which moves with the mouse.

Data – Information stored in files that is used by applications. This is differentiated from application and operating system files, which contain computer code.

Default – Standard setting unless otherwise changed.

Defrag – To run a program such as scandisk (part of Windows XP), which organizes data stored on disk for faster access.

Delete – To remove; the delete key moves one space to the right and removes whatever character is currently there.

Desktop – The starting point of Windows XP. The Desktop is what appears on the PC display when you first power on the computer. Think of it as your workspace. Many people like to customize the Desktop with a personal picture or pattern.

Dialog Box – An onscreen box that is displayed by software. These boxes are requesting/expecting some information from the user. In most cases, you must provide the information requested before continuing. Otherwise, the system will sound an error beep.

Dimmed – Not available; also called "ghosted". Menu commands and icons which are dimmed are not available for use. Usually this is due to something not being selected.

Drive – An electro-mechanical device used to read and write disks.

Directory – Another term for folder; a organizational container which holds files or other directories.

Drill Down – To navigate through folders by clicking on them.

Driver – A small application that acts as a liaison between hardware and software. Video cards, sounds cards, network cards, mice and modems require drivers.

Display – Another term for monitor; the "TV" of the computer.

Document – A specific type of data file connected with a specific application, for example, a word processing document.

Domain (name) – The unique name that identifies an Internet site , such as www.smartguypress.com.

Download – To obtain a file from another computer through the Internet. To move a file from another computer on a network to your PC.

Dragging – Moving an object by holding down the left mouse button and moving the mouse. Also refers to selecting text the same way.

DVD – An acronym for *Digital Versatile Disk*; a storage format with each disk holding at least 4.7 GB.

Ethernet – The most common type of network protocol. Most newer PCs have built in Ethernet cards.

E-mail – An electronic note sent to another computer via the Internet or other computer network. Files can be attached to e-mail messages.

Emoticons – Standard alphanumeric characters used to visually "express" emotions. Often called "smileys". For example ;-) represents a winking smiley face (turn your head slightly to the left to see this).

Extension – The last three characters of a data file name, such as mp3 or txt; identifies what application the data file is associated with. Extension viewing is turned off by default.

Field – A small box that holds information. Forms are made up of multiple fields.

File – A collection of information stored on one of more types of media. All information stored by a computer is a file of some type.

Firewall – Hardware or software that prevents unauthorized access to a PC. A "must have" if your PC is connected to the Internet via a broadband connection.

Firewire – A connection protocol for connecting peripherals to a PC. Originally developed by Apple, Firewire is renowned for its fast speed.

Folder – See directory.

Font – A specific style and type within a typeface family.

Forum – An area on a website used to post and read messages. An electronic discussion forum on virtually any topic.

Function Key – Keys found at the top of a keyboard usually labeled F1 through F12. The specific function of each key is determined by the active application. Some applications allow the user to program these keys to their desires.

GIF – *Graphic Interchange File* format. Many Internet graphics are GIF format.

Gigabyte – 1024 megabytes; abbreviated as "GB".

GUI – Acronym for *Graphical User Interface*; pronounced "gooey". This type of computer interface uses graphics, such as icons, menus, and toolbars as opposed to command-line interfaces, which use text commands.

Grouping – A new Window's feature that groups multiple open documents for one application into a single Taskbar button. Clicking the Taskbar button displays a menu for the user to select which document to make active.

Hard Disk – A electro-magnetic device for storing computer data. Hard disks are self-contained, sealed units – you can't physically see the disk. The capacity varies from ten to hundreds of gigabytes. Most PCs sold today have hard disks of 30-80 GB. Hard disk, hard drive, and hard disc all refer to the same device.

Highlighting – Also known as "selecting". Highlighting an object or text makes it active and allows it to be cut or copied. Highlighting is also required for certain application specific tools to be used.

Home Page – The initial starting web page displayed when a browser is started. The home page can always be returned to by clicking the home icon (looks like a house). The home page can be configured by the user.

Hotspot – A physical location where wireless WIFI Internet access is available. These are popping up all over, and many bookstores, cafes and airports now offer hotspots. This term can also refer to the very tip of the mouse pointer.

Hover – To hold the mouse over an icon or tool in order to display a tooltip.

HTML – An acronym for *Hypertext Markup Language*; the language used to create web pages.

Hyperlink – Text or image that when clicked on initiates an action. Hyperlink text is usually medium blue and underlined. Hyperlink graphics usually have a medium blue border around them. The mouse pointer changes to a hand with extended forefinger when hovered over a hyperlink.

Icon – A small graphic that represents something such as a folder, file, or tool.

Inactive Window – A window that is currently not available for use. Only one window can be active at any time. To make an inactive window active, click anywhere within it.

Insertion Point – A text insertion cursor; a blinking line or I-beamed shaped cursor indicating where text will appear when typing.

Internet – The world's largest computer network.

ISP – An acronym for *Internet Service Provider*; a company that provides PC owners with access to the Internet.

JPG/JPEG – A type of compressed graphic file format commonly found on the Internet.

Monitor – Another term for display; the "TV" of the computer.

Keyboard Command – See "Keyboard Shortcut" below.

Keyboard Shortcut – Keys pressed simultaneously to select menu commands, such as ctrl-c for copy.

LAN – An acronym for *Local Area Network*. Two or more computers connected via a networking protocol, such as

Ethernet.

Log In – To connect to an Internet Service Provider by providing a username and password.

Log Off – To disconnect from an Internet Service Provider. Logging in and logging off mainly apply to dial-up services.

Maximize Button – A button located in the upper right of all windows. It is the middle button. Clicking this button increases the size of the window to full-screen or, if it is already full-screen, restores the window to its original size.

Megabyte – 1024 kilobytes; a unit of measurement for computer data. Abbreviated "MB" and sometimes pronounced as "meg".

Memory – A special type of computer chip that holds computer data. See RAM and ROM.

Menu – A list of commands navigated by using the mouse Selecting these commands by clicking on them is a primary way of interacting with the computer. A way of telling the computer what you want it to do.

Menu Bar – The second line of most windows that contains menu names. Clicking the menu names displays the menu.

Microsoft Windows – A type of Operating System; the most popular operating system for personal computers.

Minimize Button – The button located in the upper right corner of a window. Looks like a dash. Clicking the minimize button shrinks a window down to an icon on the task bar. Clicking the icon on the Taskbar restores the window to its previous size.

Modem – A computer peripheral, either an external box or an internal card, that connects computers via communications lines.

Motherboard – The main circuit board of a PC.

My Computer – An icon representing all the storage devices attached to a PC.

Network – Two or more computers connected together to allow file sharing and communications.

Newsgroup – A electronic message board used to discuss various topics. A "old" part of the Internet that has largely been replaced by chat rooms and message forums.

NIC – An acronym for *Network Interface Card*. Hardware that interfaces a PC with a network.

Offline – Used to indicate "not available", either in reference to specific computer hardware or to a person being off the Internet.

OK button – A button pressed to confirm an action. Pressing the enter key is equivalent.

Online – Used to indicate "available", or connected to the Internet.

Online Service – See ISP.

Operating System – Software that controls computer hardware and user interaction. Microsoft Windows, Apple's

OS X, and Linux are the most popular operating systems in that order.

Path – A code indicating the specific storage location of a file. A path consists of a storage device, then a list of folders, then the file name.

Peripheral – An optional piece of computer hardware, such as a printer, scanner, or flash drive.

Pointer – The on-screen cursor, usually an arrow, that moves with the mouse.

Program – An executable computer file. Also called application.

RAM – Short for *Random Access Memory*. The main memory used when the computer is operating. Not to be confused with disk space.

Reboot – To power down the PC and immediately restart it.

Restart – A command accessed through Start→Turn Off Computer. Used primarily if there is a problem with the PC.

Save – A command used to write changes to a file to disk. This allows the file to be opened at a later time without losing any information.

Scanner – A external device used to create computer files from hard copy.

Scroll Bar – A movable vertical or horizontal bar located on a window that allows the user to scroll around the contents of the window.

Search Engine – A website, such as www.google.com, that provides pages of hyperlinks based on search terms.

Select – To highlight an object by clicking on it. Most commands, menu items, and tools only affect selected objects.

Serial Port – A connection socket located on a PC used to connect external devices. Rarely used anymore, as Firewire and USB are now used to connect external PC devices.

Shortcut – An icon which points to another file. Identified by a small black arrow.

Shortcut Keys – A combination of keys that when pressed, initiate a command. This is an optional way of issuing menu commands.

Shutdown – The proper way to turn off a PC. Select **Turn Off Computer**, then click the **Shutdown** button.

Software – A set of instructions used by the computer. These instructions are contained in files.

Start Menu – The main Windows menu containing access to virtually everything on a PC. Accessed through the Start button located on the bottom left of the screen.

Startup Disk – A disk containing the necessary operating system files to successfully boot the computer.

Status Bar – A bar usually located along the bottom of most application windows. This bar provides you with information about the current task at hand, such as page number, zoom size, or other statistical information.

Surf/Surfing – Using a web browser to view web pages.

Tab – A key located on the left side of the keyboard. Moves the cursor between fields. Also, when using a word processor, enters tab stops similar to those on a typewriter.

Taskbar – The horizontal bar running across the bottom of the screen. Contains buttons for each open application, as well as the Start menu and clock.

Toolbar – A horizontal or vertical bar of buttons (icons). Each button triggers a specific task.

Type Attribute – Refers to optional text effects you can apply, such as bold, italic, and underline.

Typeface – Also commonly called "font". A specific design of text.

Upload – Moving a file from your PC to another PC on a network or the Internet.

URL – *Uniform Resource Locater.* The technical name for a website address such as www.smartguypress.com.

USB – *Universal Serial Bus.* A plug and play interface between a computer and external devices, such as mice, flash drives, webcams and printers.

Virus – A small piece of software installed on your computer without your knowledge. Some viruses are not destructive and merely attempt to replicate and infect other computers. Some are very dangerous however, and could damage data on your PC.

Web – Short for *World Wide Web*. See below.

Wi-Fi – Short for *wireless fidelity*. A network transmission protocol allowing computers to connect without wires. Also know as 802.11a/b/g.

Windows – A type of operating system software developed by Microsoft Corp.

Word Processor – A software program that functions as a computer typewriter allowing the user to create, edit, and print text.

World Wide Web – A protocol of the Internet that displays information through HTML. This information, in the form of websites or web pages, is viewed by an application called a "browser".

WYSIWYG – An acronym for *What You See Is What You Get*. Pronounced as "wizzywig". Applications that display on-screen exactly how a document will print are called WYSIWYG.

Zip Disk/Zip Drive – A removable disk drive made by Iomega Corp. Before the advent of flash drives, Zip drives were very popular for making backups.

Chapter 15

Resources

Here's a list of some popular websites to get you started. Just enter the address into the address bar of your browser and hit return. Alternately, you can also surf over to www.smartguypress.com and click on **Book Links** to access this list of addresses as hyperlinks.

Search Engines

www.google.com
www.yahoo.com
www.hotbot.com
www.excite.com
www.lycos.com
www.dogpile.com

Commercial Sites

www.smartguypress.com – Cool books!
www.paypal.com
www.amazon.com
www.ebay.com
www.bn.com

Free E-mail Sites

www.yahoo.com
www.excite.com
www.hotmail.com
www.google.com

News and Current Events

www.cnn.com
www.prisonplanet.com
www.foxnews.com
www.rense.com
www.theonion.com
www.boingboing.net
www.snopes.com   Look up urban legends
www.reopen911.org
www.wingtv.net

Computer Information

www.pcworld.com
www.pcmag.com
www.cnet.com
www.whatis.com   List of file extensions.
www.slashdot.com

Free Software

www.download.com
www.tucows.com
www.openoffice.org
www.getfirefox.com

Maps and Driving Directions

www.mapquest.com
www.mapblast.com
maps.google.com

Airline Tickets and Travel

www.expedia.com
www.travelocity.com
www.priceline.com

Movies

www.imdb.com   Internet Move Database
www.moviefone.com   Reviews
movies.yahoo.com   Reviews and showtimes
www.fandango.com   Purchase advance tickets

Weather

www.wunderground com
www.weather.com

Reference Sites

www.wikipedia.com
www.dictionary.com
www.about.com

Alphabetical Index

Colophon

The word "colophon", in case you're unfamiliar with it, typically refers to the publisher's logo. It can also refer to the printer's typographical information about the specific book. However, most books don't have this type of colophon simply because most books are produced exactly the same way.

With the advent of personal computers, book design, layout, and typesetting has undergone a tremendous transformation. Work which was once done by skilled craftsmen at large book printing corporations, has now largely been replaced with PCs using specific applications.

Although this was certainly good news for those interested in printing a book, the process still required the cost of the PC and at least $2500 of software to produce the files compatible with large, commercial printing equipment.

The book-making landscape is changing once again however. The book you hold in your hands was produced with free or very low-cost software tools. How low? Less than $200!

This means that virtually anyone can now afford to publish their own book! Look for a future title from SmartGuy Press on how to do this yourself. E-mail info@smartguypress.com to be put on our mailing list.

Writing, Layout, PDF Export: OpenOffice 2.0 beta
Screen Captures: Techsmith SnagIt
Graphic Creation and Editing: Paint Shop Pro 9
Paper: 50# white offset book
Cover: 10 pt C1S, four color, layflat gloss film
Binding: Perfect

Give the Gift of Becoming a PC Expert to Your Friends and Family!

Check local or online bookstores, order directly from www.smartguypress.com, or order here

❑Yes! Please send me _____ copies of **Computer Secrets I Taught My Mom** at $18 each, plus $3 shipping per book (Illinois residents please add $1.13 sales tax per book). Canadian orders must be accompanied by a postal money order in U.S. Funds.

My check or money order for $_____ is enclosed.

Name _____

Address _____

City/State/Zip_____

E-mail _____

Make check or money order payable and return to:

SmartGuy Press
60-B W. Terra Cotta Ave
PMB 214
Crystal Lake Il 60014

Order with your credit card at www.smartguypress.com